A Treasure Hunting Text

GW00642740

Ram Publications
Hal Dawson, Editor

Modern Metal Detectors
Newly revised and profusely illustrated handbook to increase expertise and understanding of computerized or any other kind of metal detector.

Gold Panning is Easy
All new! Illustrated field guide shows the beginner exactly how to find and pan gold; follow these instructions and perform as well as any professional.

The New Successful Coin Hunting
The world's most authoritative guide to finding valuable coins, totally rewritten to include instructions for 21st Century detectors.

Treasure Recovery from Sand and Sea
Precise instructions for reaching the "blanket of wealth" beneath sands nearby and under the world's waters, totally rewritten for the 90's.

Modern Electronic Prospecting
Explains how to use a modern detector to find gold nuggets and veins of precious metal; includes instructions for panning and dredging.

Treasure from British Waters
One of Great Britain's best known detector hobbyists tells how and where he has found treasure in the waters of England and the Balearic Islands.

Treasure Hunting Pays Off
A basic introduction to all facets of treasure hunting...the equipment, the targets and the terminology; totally revised for the 21st Century detectors.

Buried Treasure of the United States
Complete field guide for finding treasure; includes state-by-state listing of thousands of sites where treasure is believed to exist.

Sunken Treasure: How to Find It
One of the world's foremost undewater salvors shares a lifetime's experience in locating and recovering treasure from deep beneath the sea.

Modern Treasure Hunting
The practical guidebook to today's metal detectors; a "how-to" manual that carefully explains the "why" of modern detector performance.

True Treasure Tales — Gar Starrett Adventures
The Secret of John Murrell's Vault
The Missing Nez Perce Gold

The New
SUCCESSFUL
COIN HUNTING

By Charles Garrett

RAM
BOOKS

ISBN 0-915920-67-0
Library of Congress Catalog Card
  No. 88-93045
The New Successful Coin Hunting
©Copyright 1989, 1992
Charles L. Garrett

Revised Printing August 1992

Book Design/Cover Photos by Mel Climer

Write for FREE listing of RAM treasure hunting books

Ram Publishing Co. • P.O. Box 38649 • Dallas, TX 75238

Once more, this book is dedicated to our special son, Charles Lewis, who incurred brain damage at an early age. Above our sorrow, we believe that perhaps God permits mental retardation in order to give mankind a glimpse of the perfect, God-created man . . . one without envy and hate within his thoughts . . . one wherein only the purest kind of love is possible.

Charles and Eleanor Garrett

If you seek God's wisdom like silver and search for it as for hidden treasures . . . you will understand righteousness, justice and equity. Happy is the man who finds wisdom and . . . understanding . . . for the gain from it is better than from silver and its profit better than gold.

Proverbs 2: 4 & 9; 3: 13-14

Contents

About the Author

Little more than a quarter century ago Charles Garrett was an electrical engineer deeply engaged in America's space effort. In his spare time he designed and built metal detectors to use in his hobby of treasure hunting. Because his detectors were obviously more effective than any available commercially, they became popular with fellow treasure hunters for whom he was soon making them. This avocation became a career when he founded Garrett Electronics to produce his inventions.

Today, the name *Garrett* stands as a synonym for the treasure hunting metal detector. Mr. Garrett himself is known as the *Grand Master Hunter,* which is also the name of his company's new computerized instrument, described as "the finest metal detector ever manufactured."

Along the way, Mr. Garrett has also become recognized as an unofficial spokesman for the hobby of treasure hunting and the metal detecting industry through a long list of honors, personal appearances and books. He is the author of several major works which have been accepted as veritable "texts" for treasure hunting. In addition, he began publication of the popular line of *Garrett Guides* last year. These modestly priced pocket-size books are designed to be carried by treasure hunters for actual use in the field. Eight titles already in the series cover a wide range of topics, with *Guides* on additional subjects forthcoming.

Another significant contribution is his introduction of Gar Starrett, a metal detecting hero who was featured in a recent first novel, *The Secret of John Murrell's Vault.* The author reports that we can expect to hear a lot more about Gar and his exploits!

Mr. Garrett has explained that his writing began almost accidentally. "In the early days of Garrett, when I spent considerable time traveling around the country to present seminars and other programs," he explains, "people would ask for written copies of my presentations. These were my first 'works' that Ram published."

Successful Coin Hunting was the first major work written and published by Charles Garrett. For over 15 years it has been hailed as the premier guidebook for the hobby of coin hunting with a metal detector.

Ram itself has grown along with Garrett Electronics and now publishes a broad list of books related to treasure hunting and metal detectors.

Charles Garrett was born and reared in the "piney woods" of Deep East Texas where tales of hidden treasure made small town life more livable during the Depression. After service in the U.S. Navy during the Korean Conflict, he earned an engineering degree from Lamar State University.

He is married to the former Eleanor Smith of Pennington, Texas, who has played a key role in the growth and development of Garrett Electronics. They have two sons and a daughter.

As a graduate engineer and a businessman, Charles Garrett introduced discipline to the manufacture of metal detectors. He has generally raised the standards of metal detecting everywhere, as the hobby has grown from a haphazard pastime to almost a science. He has used a metal detector of his own design to search for and find treasure on every continent except Antarctica. He has also scanned under the lakes, seas and oceans of the world.

Presentation of *The NEW Successful Coin Hunting* by the Grand Master Hunter represents another milestone for both him and the hobby of hunting for coins with a metal detector.

Hal Dawson, Editor
Ram Publishing Co.

Winter, 1989

Foreword

Over 15 years ago when I was asked to write the Foreword to the first edition of *Successful Coin Hunting,* I refused. That's right! I told Charles and his editor that there were dozens of highly qualified writers who could do a much better job. Still, they persisted. Charles said that he knew that I would be honest and straightforward.

He didn't realize it then that he thus provided me with words which still describe him to a "T." My endorsement of Charles and his first book on coin hunting represented no mere testimonial or praise afforded to a best friend. It was simply credit given where credit was due.

I described Charles as "beyond doubt the most respected authority on advanced metal detecting equipment in the field today," and I discussed his recent achievement of being named Manufacturer of the Year by America's treasure hunters. In pointing out why Charles was unique among manufacturers, I noted that "most manufacturers are primarily engineering experts, devoting their time to design and production."

Charles, even now, continues to go beyond laboratory design. "It is indeed a rarity," I observed, "to see an electronic specialist who is also one of today's most successful coin hunters, prospectors and all-around treasure seekers. Additionally, Charles has left his mark on the metal detector industry with numerous inventions."

It's somewhat amusing to me today when I realize that the detectors that we were all praising so highly 15 years ago are now little more than relics. Yes, we treasure hunters have gone through two entire generations of electronic metal detectors in less than one and one-half decades. From the BFO's, through the TR's and the primitive VLF's to today's advanced automated VLF's and the computerized instruments that feature microprocessor controls.

These totally new instruments are but one of the reasons that Charles found it necessary to rewrite this fine book. But, I'll let him tell you about that. I've read the new book, and it's a dandy! There's so much I'd like to say about it...to let you know how much it can help any of you...to describe the vast improvement it represents over any other book ever written on coin-hunting...even by Charles himself!

The best way that I know how to do all of this, however, is simply to repeat three paragraphs from my Foreword to that long-ago First Edition in the early 1970's when I described the book as one...

"...that will astonish you and challenge your imagination. It will help both the beginner or professional gain knowledge on 'where' and 'how.' Charles has gone beyond other writers in the field of coin hunting in the amount and quality of specific information he has set down. In addition to his own knowledge he also shares many, many tips, ideas and pictures from other experienced and professional coin seekers from all parts of the country. The book is filled with excellent photographs showing actual finds and individual hunting methods. By combining his extensive knowledge of electronic equipment with his long experience in the fascinating hobby of coin hunting, Charles has been able to produce a masterpiece of instructive literature—a classic book in the field that may never be surpassed.

"If I sound biased and impressed by (this book), I intend to! When you have read your copy, you will understand why. You will recommend it enthusiastically to your friends as the most complete and comprehensive coin hunting manual you have ever read.

"I thank Charles for the opportunity to write this introduction. I am proud to be a part of this book and to count myself among the millions who have the honor of knowing this unselfish and humble man, my friend, Charles Garrett."

Since I wrote those words, Charles and I have experienced so many more grand times together. We've hunted for countless treasures...and, even found a few of them! As our friendship has deepened, my admiration and respect for him have grown more intense.

And, my, how the detectors themselves have changed! When I can *hear* the new Grand Master Hunter CX III telling me how deep a target is buried or when I "notch" a GTA to find just one kind of target, I don't miss the old instruments with their hit-or-miss circuitry at all. You newcomers to the hobby don't know how lucky you are to have this fine equipment.

Yet so much about the hobby hasn't changed. And, Charles Garrett understands both the old and the new because he has truly seen it all as far as detectors are concerned.

So, when I reread my words written so long ago and marvel at this totally new book with its keen insight into modern detector usage and its magnificent color pictures, I can add but one word...Amen!

Finally, to Charles again must go my deep appreciation for allowing me to participate in this outstanding achievement in treasure hunting.

Roy Lagal

Lewiston, Idaho
Summer 1992

In England or wherever he is, Charles Garrett can be found hunting with a metal detector, a vocation and hobby that has taken him around the world.

Author's Note

The following three paragraphs are reprinted exactly as they were written in 1973 to answer the question . . . Why Did I Write *Successful Coin Hunting?*:

"I wrote this book because I want to pass on to you, the coin hunter, the things I have learned about coin hunting. I believe the beginning coin hunter should learn as much as possible about the hobby before starting out. I hope that this book will give you a head start down the road of successful coin hunting.

"Perhaps some of the information included will not seem particularly valuable to the seasoned coin hunter. Many coin hunters are more active and experienced than I. Nevertheless, some of the tips and techniques may be of value to these persons. Discussions of the different detector types, their operations and applications may benefit even the 'old salt.' Several basic types of coin hunting detectors are on the market, but to my knowledge there is no complete guidebook which explains all the different instruments, their peculiarities and operating characteristics, and how they are best suited for the many different coin hunting applications.

"So, my purpose is this: to help all *new* coin hunters become *successful* coin hunters. To them I offer my 20-plus years of 'know how,' 'where to' and 'when to' coin hunting knowledge. To the already experienced and successful coin hunters I offer possibly a few new coin hunting tips, but, more fittingly, my total sympathy for those breaking backs that remind us all of the successful coin hunting days we have had. To all detector operators

Multitudes of coins are waiting to be found by any hobbyist who is willing to learn what it takes to become successful with a metal detector.

I offer the detector knowledge related to coin hunting that I have gained from the building, testing and use of detectors in coin hunting."

Now we're well into the 1990s!

All of the above remains true, except that my experience has been increased by some 20 or more years in the field, engineering laboratory and marketplace. Plus, the detectors on the market today that have come out of our laboratory are vastly different from the ones referred to in the above paragraphs. More experience and new detectors...those two facts are the primary reasons I give when fellow treasure hunters ask why I want to revise such a popular book as *Successful Coin Hunting.* (Some say how *dare* I revise it!)

The experience I have gained and the experiences that so many of you have shared with me—plus the completely new instruments available to coin hunters today—make a complete rewriting of the book absolutely necessary.

For, you see, the manual has already been "revised" several times. Many readers do not realize that each time a Ram book is reprinted, its editors study the text carefully to make certain that all information on equipment and techniques is as current as possible. In the fast moving technology of today's world substantial alterations are often required. Yet, what changes can I or any other writer make in describing BFO or TR detectors? No matter how much we loved those old instruments, they're obsolete today. Anyone who insists on using them must realize that he (or she) is placing severe limitations on the ability to find treasure!

It's time for a new book on coin hunting!

Fans of the old volume will find much here that they remember. Neither the physical laws nor the mythical lore of treasure hunting has changed. Many of the ideas and stories from the old book are just as applicable in the mid-1990s as they were in the early 1970s. I trust that newcomers to our hobby will enjoy this material and learn from it as so many others tell me they have.

There's also much that's totally new in this *Treasure*

Hunting Text because ever-advancing technology makes our venerable hobby as modern as tomorrow.

I speak especially of our new Garrett Grand Master Hunter CX III detector and the magnificent Ultra GTA instruments. When they ushered in the 1990s, the GTA's with their precise notch discrimination and easy-to-understand LCD presentation of all target information immediately became the world's most popular detectors for hunting coins. And, what can I or anyone else tell you about the CX III that its own *TreasureTalk™* can't say better. This is truly a detector that speaks for itself!

So, to the treasure hunters of the world I once more present *The NEW Successful Coin Hunting*. Whether your detector be a Grand Master Hunter CX III or an Eagle...a 1265 or a GTA...a Sabre or an Ace, I sincerely hope that this new book will enable each of you to achieve as much pleasure...as much sheer delight from coin hunting with a metal detector as I have enjoyed since the 1950's. And, perhaps sometime when we're both finding coins with a Green Machine...

I'll see you in the field!

Charles Garrett

Garland, Texas
Summer 1992

Chapter 1
To Begin With

Coin hunting is simply the searching for and retrieving of lost coins. Countless millions of coins have been lost and await recovery by the metal detector hobbyist. Thousands of Indianhead and Wheat pennies, Buffalo nickels, Barber dimes, Liberty and Washington quarters, Liberty-walking half dollars and many other types of silver coins are being recovered . . . all around us . . . every day. Surprising numbers of *gold* coins continue to be found these many years after they were in wide circulation. And, it appears people have always lost more coins than have ever been found . . . even by hobbyists who are now using the most modern metal detectors!

Coins are lost everywhere people go. Coins are being found everywhere people have been. These facts support the reasons why this aspect of treasure hunting is believed to be the fastest growing hobby in America.

Many persons not familiar with the hobby of coin hunting find it difficult to believe that coins can actually be *found* . . . that they are lost and just waiting to respond to the electronic signals of a metal detector.

"Who loses coins?" they ask. "Surely there are not enough lost coins to make it worth while to buy a metal detector, then to spend time looking for them!" An appropriate reply is that any active and experienced coin hunter can easily find 5,000 coins each year. That's right, *five thousand!*

How do I arrive at this figure? This is an average of 100 coins found each weekend for 50 weeks . . . a goal that I consider reasonable and easily obtainable . . . based on personal experience . . . and on my first-hand knowledge of the success of thousands of other coin hunters.

How It's Done

On any given weekend an experienced coin hunter can find from 100 to 500 coins. This same hobbyist, however, would not find any coins in this same length of time if he did not follow the rules that will be explained in this *Treasure Hunting Text*. A coin hunter must search for coins where they have been lost, and he must search for them in the proper manner. No barriers of age or sex exist in this great hobby. After only a short time, anyone can learn how to search for coins and discover the best places to find them. Believe me, there are literally thousands of "best places." You'll soon discover that only you know about some of these.

For example, my father and I found more than 250 coins in an area 18 feet square at the site of an old drive-in movie theater. We recovered these coins from the small area immediately in front of the projection booth in a period of less than 90 minutes. Around the perimeter of this area a pipe railing had been built to keep persons from walking in front of the images being projected toward the screen. Apparently, this railing drew children (of all ages) like a magnet. They must have climbed on it, swung from it, played on it and performed every manner of gymnastics.

Dad and I found the majority of our coins directly beneath this metal fence and on both sides within an area of approximately two feet. Sometimes the coins were found in bunches as we dug up clumps of dirt. When I made the first sweep with my Garrett, its speaker sang out, "Zip, zip, zip, zip, zip!" and I thought, "There certainly are a lot of pulltabs here." All of these "zips," however, were "the sound of money!"

Other Successes

This is but a single example of the success that can be obtained by any coin hunter. And, there's an immediate obvious monetary value to each discovery! In addition, many coins commonly found in old areas are worth several times their face denomination. Many times I have heard of just a single coin worth enough to more than pay for the detector that discovered it. Occasionally, just a single coin is recovered and found to be worth thousands of dollars.

But, other pleasures can be just as rewarding as the financial. There's a special "value" in rediscovering a moment of the past. Just think . . . each time a coin is lost, a moment in life's passage is preserved until someone finds that coin. When you dig up an old coin that your detector has located, you're literally holding the past in your hand.

Ask any long-time coin hunter what he thinks of the hobby . . . why he or she spends leisure time searching with a metal detector. You will find unanimous support in favor of this rewarding hobby. Health benefits come right along with the monetary returns . . . the sheer fun of getting exercise in the fresh air and sunshine. In fact, the main reason I search for treasure and hunt coins is that I am primarily interested in these health benefits I receive. When I find coins and other valuables, I consider them the added benefits of treasure hunting . . . the frosting on the cake!

As described in this chapter, Wayne Garrett, the author's father, recovers just one of the many coins they found in front of the projection booth at an old, deserted drive-in movie.

Just how successful each coin hunter is will depend to a large extent on where he or she hunts. Equally as important is how carefully the detecting instrument has been selected and how well the hobbyist has mastered its use. There are literally dozens of different brands and models of instruments from which to choose. Most of these can be grouped into only a handful of categories. Each of these categories deserves the individual attention and discussion that will be given in this text.

Anyone seriously interested in coin hunting is urged to study these discussions, especially those related to the type of instrument you are now using. There are many "tricks" and techniques that a coin hunter must know in order to receive maximum benefits and results from using a metal detector. Vast improvements have been made in these instruments in just a few years. The technology of the 1960s that we considered so superior when the first edition of this book was published is totally obsolete today. And, the advances of the past two years have made more recent technology from the 1970's equally as obsolete. As for the technology of the early 1980's . . . well, very little of it is still on "the cutting edge."

I say to you successful coin hunters who are happy today with an older detector: so be it; hunt in good health! Let me urge you, however, to study the newer models and learn about their capabilities. No matter how much ability and expertise you possess, *you'll never dig up a coin that your detector's circuitry can't find!*

To you newcomers to the hobby I implore you to start out right with a modern detector . . . perhaps, even investing more than you had planned. And, I urge you to work smarter as well as harder. You must learn how to use your detector properly. Success for any hobbyist comes only in direct proportion to the amount of time and study devoted to developing the proper skills with an instrument.

Well, let's get started. I'm happy you're coming along with me to participate in this great adventure of coin hunting. We will venture from the ocean depths to mountain peaks . . . from the snow to the desert. Coin hunting is fun and rewarding. You'll see!

Chapter 2

Coin Hunters' Traits

Who hunts coins?

Every metal detector hobbyist. The answer is that simple and easy. At Garrett Electronics we know that *every* detector that we sell will be used at one time or another to hunt coins and that a vast majority (some estimate as high as 70%) will be used to hunt little else.

So, every hobbyist is a coin hunter . . . at least, some of the time. But, what distinguishes the *real* coin hunters from all the others? What do *successful* coin hunters have that the others don't have? Because of my lengthy experience in metal detecting, I'm usually able to spot these successful coin hunters pretty quickly. And, their success can be obvious to me at a THing club meeting or the National Federation banquet. I don't have to examine a coin hunter's collection or watch his or her technique in the field to recognize success.

How can these *winners* be spotted so easily? Once again, the answer is simple. I just look for a few character traits . . . a few signs that tell me about a person's intensity . . . a few mannerisms that symbolize success. In short, I look for *hallmarks of an effective coin hunter.* Let me try to explain what I believe they are and explain how you can achieve them.

1. Desire

This must come first . . . and it may not come easily. But, don't force desire on yourself. Let it begin as just a thorough study of metal detecting and coin hunting to learn the rewards that can be enjoyed from the hobby. Soon, you will come to know and understand the successes that others have experienced as you learn the major coinages and gain an understanding of them. From such studies you'll cultivate a *feeling* for coin hunting . . . a desire to be successful in this field. You'll know . . . but, more importantly, you'll *believe* . . . that great rewards

17

can and will be yours. Only then can you really begin to generate a desire that will carry you through the learning phase and keep you interested . . . and successful . . . all the rest of your life.

2. Research

With a desire to succeed in coin hunting, you'll come to love the research necessary to achieve the greatest success. Of course, it helps tremendously if you already enjoy history and appreciate stories of the past . . . because that's what coin hunting research is all about. It's a study of history to learn where people have been! That's where you'll find coins. Modern day parks yield thousands of currently circulated coins. And, it's true . . . they're fun to find. But, when you dig your first 1850 gold coin in an old settlers' campground that *you* discovered through research . . . that's when a spark will ignite that will never be extinguished.

3. Choosing Proper Equipment

The challenge of equipping yourself properly is one that every succesful coin hunter must meet and answer through diligent – and continuing – application. You will soon find that there are many different kinds of metal detectors, most of which you should investigate. Be particularly thorough in your survey of the coin hunting instruments. Study all manufacturers' literature. Ask successful coin hunters about *their* detectors. Talk to dealers and ask questions of them. Join a treasure hunting club and observe its other members. Ask questions about their equipment. Read every book and magazine article on detectors that you see. Then, carefully analyze your findings. If a manufacturer says his detector is the one you should buy, find out how successful *that manufacturer* has been with his own equipment. Visit metal detector shops to pick up and test various models. Make sure you see an *outdoor* demonstration . . . better yet, *you* participate in the demonstration yourself. Bench tests are fine, but you're not going to find any coins there. Only after you've gotten *your* hands on the various models you like can you make a final, intelligent choice.

4. Using Equipment Properly

This comes next . . . before anything else. Applying yourself diligently and with great patience, learn the basic controls of your new detector. Try to understand what the various functions

One of the "greats" of metal detecting, the late L. L. "Abe" Lincoln displays some of the many valuable coins he recovered from old mining camps. Many, also shown below, are gold.

and modes are . . . learn when and how they should be used. Study your Owner's Manual and all instruction tapes that are available . . . not just once or twice, but many times. Before you ever turn on your detector in the field, go through its complete operation mentally. Then, take pen in hand and *write out the procedures.* Can you do this? Only when you have memorized and can write out the instructions for your detector, can you expect to understand them properly. Finally, take your Owner's Manual into the field and study it as you experiment with your new detector to make certain you are operating the controls properly.

5. Developing Faith

Now that you have chosen the proper equipment and learned how to use it, you must develop faith in it. Even more important, you must develop faith in *yourself!* Never deviate from the belief that *you will be successful!* This trait cannot be stressed strongly enough. You must always have faith in yourself and your abilities with your detector to produce results beyond the wildest dreams of your imagination. Only if you expect success will you achieve it!

6. Learning Patience

The importance of this trait, too, cannot be overemphasized. Patience is truly a key to success. There will be days . . . perhaps several in succession . . . when you will not be successful. You'll sometimes wonder why you bother to turn on your detector. Just remember that even the most successful treasure hunters come home empty-handed at times. Do *they* consider such a day unproductive? Not on your life! I've been treasure hunting for more than 40 years now, and I can tell you truthfully that each time I take a detector into the field, I learn something new . . . about the detector . . . about the hobby . . . and about life. So, a day in which you find few – or no – coins can truly be a stepping stone . . . a time to perfect your skills (see below) for the many days to come when you *will* be successful. And, as Gar Starrett, fictional hero of our hobby says, "Every treasure hunt is a genuine pleasure . . . if nobody gets hurt or spends money he or she can't afford."

7. Adapting to Conditions

No two coin hunting locations are alike. The soil, its mineral content and moisture, its surface condition, history of the area, trash and treasure buried there . . . these and many other factors determine the nature of each location. With the experience gained from searching many different sites, you'll be able to size up any new area quickly. Then, the expertise you have developed with your equipment will enable you to make the proper adjustments, determine the most effective scanning techniques and be able to analyze all targets before you dig. The flexibility to adapt is an absolute essential to success.

8. Concentrating

You must become one with your site and concentrate on giving 100% of your mental and physical effort to searching for coins. Without total concentration you'll be deaf to the whispers of signals that alert the successful hobbyist to deeply buried and

Charles Garrett has searched for coins all over the world. Here he is shown seeking coins, relics and caches with an early detector in the ruins of a century-old South American city.

valuable coins. Without total concentration you'll ignore those telltale detector signals produced by coins buried amongst junk targets. Without total concentration coins will literally hide themselves from you. When you concentrate fully on coin hunting, however, anything will be possible!

9. Perfecting Your Skills

This must be a continuing challenge! Let your detector become *your eyes and ears.* It will never lie to you. When your detector produces a signal, *something* caused that signal to be made. Let nothing your detector reports . . . through sound or meter . . . escape you. Perfect your skills through learning about your detector's capabilities, characteristics and limitations. Learn to visualize what's in the ground before you dig. When your detector signals a target, ask yourself some questions. What is it? How big is it? How deep? How is it lying in the ground? What is its shape? Then dig the target and answer your questions as you recover it. How did you do? Did you guess right? Or, did you fail in one or more areas? Try to analyze your errors and learn where you went wrong. If you'll try this through just a hundred recoveries, you'll be amazed how accurate you have become at identifying detected targets.

10. Developing Proper Recovery Techniques

By learning correct digging methods, you will double your recovery speed. You'll virtually eliminate the chance of damaging valuable coins. And, of equal importance, you will learn easy ways to restore the area where you have dug to the condition in which you found it. Always strive to *improve* the condition of a search area, and leave no trail to let anyone know you have dug there.

11. Expanding Your Skills

In addition to coins there are many other kinds of treasure just waiting to be found with a metal detector. Prepare yourself to find this wealth! The day may come when you learn where a money cache is hidden. Or, you may get the chance to search for nuggets in gold country. Be able to take advantage of these opportunities. As you become proficient in coin hunting, study the numerous professionally written treasure hunting books – but concentrate not only on coin hunting. You should at least become "bookwise" to cache and relic hunting, ghost-towning, prospecting and recovery from beach, surf and underwater locations. All of the knowledge is there for you, written by experts with several lifetimes of experience. Take advantage of this knowledge so easily available from those who have learned the attributes and traits of *other* types of treasure hunters. Be prepared when the opportunity knocks, and, remember that you'll never learn *all there is to know* about coin hunting or any other phase of metal detecting. So, always be ready to learn from others about the effective metal detector techniques they have developed. Then, apply these newly learned techniques to your searching!

12. Ethical Treasure Hunting

In Chapter 14 of this book you'll find the *Metal Detector Operators Code of Ethics.* Study this code, learn all that it means and apply these rules to your everyday searching. You'll be protecting our hobby, and you'll be protecting your own digging rights and sites. Don't take these rules lightly. They have been developed over years of study by professional treasure hunters and long-time hobbyists who recognize the value that comes from protecting and insuring the future of metal detecting.

What a grand and glorious hobby coin hunting can be . . . for men and women, boys and girls . . . coins are waiting to found anywhere people have been!

Chapter 3
For All Ages

Coin hunting is, indeed, a perfect hobby for all ages! Young and old, men and women, the robust and the handicapped . . . all can find coins with equal success when they are using quality metal detectors.

As you become more active in the search for coins, you will encounter fellow hobbyists ranging from youngsters just three or four to senior citizens more than 80 years young. There is no age limit! Coin hunting is popular because it is fun and rewarding. Even though detectors have been around for many years now, only during the past decade or so has coin hunting really found its place in the outdoor hobby world. As its popularity has grown, so has the broad range of people who enjoy it.

Coin hunting can serve as the perfect hobby to involve the entire family. Each member can participate. Even with only one detector all can combine their talents . . . provided no one individual is assigned all the digging tasks! Of course, it's far better when more than one detector is available, so that everyone can experience the thrill of initial discovery.

Over the years I have watched all of this happen. I've seen

Above
Hunting coins with a metal detector is truly a universal hobby. Men and women of all ages can enjoy it equally and participate in its benefits.
Below
What a world of metallic objects lie beneath the soil just waiting for a metal detector! Beginners will be amazed at how their collections grow.

wives become as avid coin hunters as husbands, and I've
enjoyed watching children begin to join in. In fact, I've known
some families in which the children were more successful coin
hunters than their parents. Perhaps it's their sharp ears, or
maybe they just have more persistence and the other traits of a
coin hunter explained in the preceding chapter.

Why They Hunt

Primarily, people hunt coins for the simple fun of the hobby, as
well as for the relaxation and good exercise they get. It gives
them something interesting to do and brings a little *mystery* into
their everyday existences. Yes, mystery! The coin hunter never
knows what will be found until a target is uncovered! Searching
for coins with a metal detector is relaxing, both mentally and
physically, and is also rewarding in many other ways.

More and more campers, hunters, fishermen, vacationers
and back-packers are adding a metal detector to their normal
sports gear. They have chosen to let coin hunting and other
forms of searching with metal detectors fill gaps in their regular
outdoor activities, providing added enjoyment for them as well
as for other members of their families.

Sure, dad is an avid fisherman. He can't get enough of casting
or just watching a cork bob around. When mother and the children get restive, they can turn on their metal detector(s) and
"fish" for their own targets. When the "real" fish aren't biting,
dad will often want to join them. It's amazing what there is to be
found with a metal detector at a popular old fishing hole!

It's Profitable!

Of course, there is an immediate financial reward with each
coin found. And, coin hunting will ultimately prove to be "profitable" for any persistent hobbyist. He or she will be surprised
how soon they find coins with enough value to pay for their metal
detector. For this reason searching for coins is by far the most
popular aspect of the overall hobby of treasure hunting. Of
course, it is also popular because coins can be sought – and found
– almost anywhere. Expensive and time-consuming trips to
ghost towns, prospecting country or oceanside beaches are not

necessary. The nearby neighborhood park or schoolyard can provide both adventure and rewards.

Individuals who have no interest at all in seeking large hidden treasures become dedicated to coin hunting. Many of these individuals, however, gradually extend their new hobby into other areas of treasure hunting. They become relic and cache hunters; they seek nuggets as electronic prospectors; they find themselves proficient beach hunters simply by taking their detector along on the family's vacation at the coast.

Over the years, we have watched with pleasure as the "old pro" treasure hunter of yesterday has been steadily replaced by the everyday hobbyist. Why has this happened? Because hunting with a metal detector is one of the most fascinating and interesting pastimes ever to capture the imagination of the world . . . no matter what targets are sought or found!

It's Healthy!

Many people enjoy coin hunting because it is an easy and perfect way to achieve and maintain physical fitness. One of the

These tiny, but very valuable, ancient coins are typical of those found by Charles Garrett while hunting in England where old Roman coins and those from other cultures abound.

most valuable fringe benefits of the metal detecting hobby pertains to health. Regular use of a metal detector insures a continual body-building program.

The individual who is not in good physical condition at the outset of the hobby soon feels leg muscles building up and sees flab around the waist diminishing as the spare tire is deflated. Breathing improves, and the heart beats more steadily. And, after a vigorous day of searching in the field, is it any wonder that hobbyists sleep bett r than their friends who sit and watch?

Coin hunting can be excellent therapy for many who are recovering from an operation, illness or injury. Certainly the level of activity must be governed by a patient's physical condition, but this hobby can take convalescents out of doors into fresh air and sunshine. Listening to the hum of a metal detector will also permit their minds to soar far above morbid thoughts of the sickroom. Who can worry about illness or injury when thinking about discovering a valuable old coin?

We know of many cases of individuals who have rapidly recuperated from long illnesses and operations when they earnestly began the hobby of coin hunting. Even those with heart problems . . . especially those who require exercise with some constraint . . . find coin hunting just the ticket for the exact kind of workout they need.

This subject of health is discussed in much greater length in Chapter 16.

It's Popular!

It's been estimated that at least 90% of all detector owners hunt coins at one time or another, and I am confident that every Garrett detector ever sold has been or will be used to hunt for coins at least occasionally in its service life. Approximately 60% of all metal detector hobbyists use their instruments almost entirely for coin hunting and rarely get involved in seeking any other kinds of treasure with them.

Some coin hunters – I've estimated as high as 20% – become so adept at the hobby that they could be called "professionals." They spend most of their free time searching for coins and looking for places to hunt. How many coin hunters are women? I used to estimate 30%, but this percentage could be low. I know that the number of women enjoying the hobby is steadily increasing.

There are no finer people than today's coin hunters – or, treasure hunters, for that matter. I have come to know literally thousands of these wonderful people, and I am convinced they are among the best. They possess all of the worthwhile traits I outlined in the preceding chapter, but most important of all they are hard-working people who enjoy the rewards of their own labors. They appreciate nature and the out-of-doors and truly understand the meaning of a good day's work and the rewards that it can bring.

Believe me when I tell you that treasure hunters are here to stay!

This old ghost town near Anaconda, CO, has been searched many times, yet new detectors with deeper-seeking and more sensitive circuitry locate prizes that earlier models overlooked.

Chapter 4

How It Works

I n trying to explain how a metal detector operates I've said many times that there's no "magic" to the way it can so easily locate a coin in the grass, buried deeply in soil or rocks or in the surf. It's all a matter of electronics. That's what I *say.*

But, yet . . . there's a bit of "magic" there, too, for every avid coin hunter. In point of fact, a metal detector might simply be an electronic device that detects the presence of metal, primarily through the transmission and reception of radio wave signals. When you're scanning it across a spot of ground, and it makes a noise that alerts you to the presence of a coin several inches below the surface . . . don't say it isn't magic!

But, let's consider for a minute just what a metal detector is and how it works. To start, let's consider what it is *not.* A metal detector is not an instrument (geiger counter) that detects energy emissions from radioactive materials. It is not an instrument (magnetometer) that measures the intensity of magnetic fields. It does not "point" to coins or any other kind of metal; it does not measure the abundance of metal. A metal detector simply detects its presence and reports this fact.

When a coin is made of metal – and, most of them usually are – a metal detector can signal the location of this coin a reasonable distance beneath its searchcoil. How all this comes about is a somewhat more complicated story.

Knowing how a gasoline engine operates really doesn't make you a better driver. Similarly, it isn't necessary to understand the scientific principles of metal detection for you to be able to find coins with a detector. But, we all know that understanding an internal combustion engine and knowing a little about how it makes the wheels turn helps you become a better *operator* of a motor vehicle. In the same manner, understanding the how and why of metal detection results in a better *coin hunter.* Since *bet-*

ter coin hunters find *more* coins, it would be well if every hobbyist had some understanding of the basic scientific principles of metal detection. So, here we go, to explain in laymen's language just how a metal detector locates coins as well as all other metal.

By Radio Waves

Like any other metal object, a coin is detected essentially by the transmission and reception of radio wave signals. This is the scientific "principle" that governs operation of all metal detectors. If they're all the same, you may quickly ask, why do some cost so much more? What distinguishes quality metal detectors such as those manufactured by Garrett from those that don't seem to find many coins or much of anything? Primarily, it's the methods by which the detectors transmit signals and the sophistication with which the signals are received and interpreted. In a word, it's the circuitry.

When a radio signal is produced in the searchcoil of any metal detector, an electromagnetic field is generated that flows out into the surrounding medium, whether it be earth, rock, water, wood, air or any other material. This electromagnetic field doesn't particularly seek coins or any other kind of metal; it just flows out into the air, earth, water or whatever medium is present. But, the "lines" of this electromagnetic field penetrate metal whenever it comes within the pattern of the detection path. The extent of this pattern depends to a large degree upon the power used to transmit the signal and the resistance of the medium into which the signal is transmitted.

The electromagnetic field generated by transmission from a detector's searchcoil causes something called "eddy currents" to flow on coins detected by this field. Generating these currents on the coin causes a loss of power in the electromagnetic field and this power loss is sensed by the detector's circuitry. Electromagnetic field lines passing through a coin and generating eddy currents on it distort the normal electromagnetic field. This distortion is one of the clues that alert a detector to the nearby presence of metal.

These currents and the resulting distortion of the electromagnetic field are sensed by a metal detector. Simultaneously, eddy currents on the coin generate a secondary electromagnetic field into the surrounding medium, which gives the detector still another clue. A receiver in the searchcoil detects these signals at the same time the loss of generating power is being detected. Circuitry of the metal detector *simultaneously* interprets all these sensations and generates appropriate signals to the operator. The detection device instantly reports that a coin (or, some sort of metal) appears to be present.

Intricate Circuitry

If you think all this interpreting and generating requires complicated electronic circuitry, you're right . . . especially for a detector that expects to detect deeply. That's just one of the reasons for the vast differences in the quality – and prices – of metal detectors. Those instruments with more sophisticated circuitry designed to do a better job of sending out signals and then receiving and interpreting them for you simply cost more to develop and manufacture.

But, they find more coins!

Electromagnetic signals from the detector's searchcoil cause

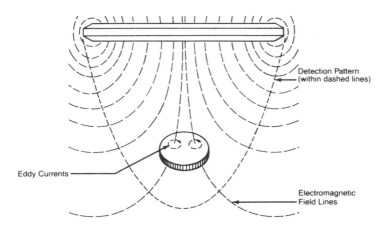

When any metal comes within the detection pattern of a searchcoil, "eddy currents" flow over its surface, resulting in loss of power which the detector's circuits can sense.

eddy currents to flow on the surface of any metal object (or mineral) having the ability to conduct electricity. Precious metals such as silver, copper and gold have higher conductivities and, appropriately, more flow of eddy current than iron, foil, tin or other less desirable metals. Since metal detectors can "measure" the amount of power that is used to generate eddy currents, the detector can "tell" which metals are the better conductors.

Quite simply, the quality of signals generated, received and interpreted by the metal detector and the ability of the coin hunter to act upon them determines the difference between "digging junk" and finding coins.

Oh, that it could be so simple!

Penetration of the electromagnetic field into the "search matrix" (that area over which a metal detector scans) is described as "coupling." Such coupling can be "perfect" into air, fresh water, wood, glass and certain non-mineralized earth.

Unfortunately, life is seldom perfect. The search matrix which a metal detector "illuminates" (through transmission and reception of signals) contains many elements and minerals – some detectable and some not, some desirable and some not. A metal detector's electronic response at any given instant is caused by *all* conductive metals and minerals and ferrous non-conductive minerals illuminated in the search matrix by the electromagnetic field. Detection of minerals is, in most cases, undesirable.

And, wouldn't you know it? Two of the most undesirable are also two of the most common: natural iron (ferrous minerals) found in most of the earth's soil and wetted salt found in much of the earth's soil and water. Not only do these minerals produce detection signals, but they inhibit the ability of instruments to detect metal.

When iron minerals are present within the search matrix, the electromagnetic field is upset and signals are distorted. Iron mineral detection, therefore, presents a major problem to manufacturers and users of metal detectors. Although detection of such minerals may be desirable when a prospector is seeking ferrous black sand or magnetite that could contain gold or silver; it is a nuisance to the hobbyist who is looking for coins.

A primary design criterion of any detector, therefore, must be to filter or eliminate responses from undesirable elements, informing the treasure hunter only of those from coins and other desirable objects. This is accomplished in a variety of ways depending upon the type of metal detector.

Such words as ground balancing, ground canceling, discrimination and elimination are used moreorless interchangeably to describe the ability of a detector to seek out only desirable targets while ignoring ground minerals, trash and junk.

It is in this area that many of the significant advances have been – and continue to be – made in the design of metal detectors. Electronic engineers have long known that this task could be accomplished through various methods of circuitry which properly manage the normal electrical phase relationship among resistive, inductive and conductive voltage.

Now, simple phase shifting itself is a phonomenon basic to the understanding of electricity. It's the management of it that makes detectors so different from each other. Management of this phase shifting to enable a specific metal detector to "dial

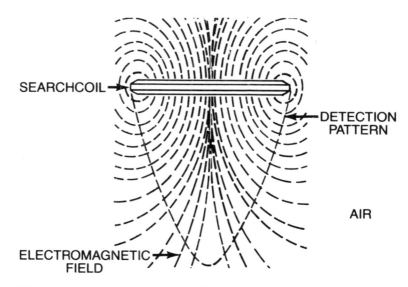

"Coupling" describes penetration of a detector's electromagnetic field into any object near the transmitter antenna. Perfect coupling as shown can result in air, fresh water and wood.

out" iron mineralization or other undesirable targets, while still permitting the discovery of coins, involves highly proprietary knowledge and circuitry protected by U.S. patents. The author and other Garrett engineers, incidentally, hold a number of these patents, including some that are primary in the manufacture of metal detectors.

Depth of Detection

The electromagnetic field transmitted by any detector flows into the search matrix, generating eddy currents on the surface of conductive substances. Detectable targets that sufficiently disturb the field are detected. But, why, you may ask, do some detectors detect deeper than others? And, for goodness sakes, why do *some* detectors even detect better targets than others?

The answer is simple. The *better* detectors detect deeper and they will reject unacceptable targets. Circuitry of these *better* detectors is more intricate, enabling it to penetrate deeper into the soil by avoiding unwanted targets. Not only will this circuitry project a stronger electromagnetic field, it is designed to interpret disturbances in this field with more precision. Of course, the materials present in the search matrix further determine how deep the electromagnetic field will penetrate.

Of the factors that determine how deeply a target can be detected only the electromagnetic field and the circuitry to interpret its disturbances are a function of the detector. Two other important factors, size and surface area, are determined by the target itself.

Surface Area

Simply stated, the larger a metal target . . . the better and more deeply it can be detected. Larger detection signals come from targets that produce more eddy currents. An object with double the surface area of another will produce detection signals twice as strong as those of the smaller object, but it will not necessarily be detected twice as far. It is true, however, that a large target will produce the same detection signal as a small target positioned closer to the searchcoil.

Generally speaking, modern metal detectors are *surface area* detectors. They are not metallic volume (mass) detectors. How a detector "sees" a target will be determined to a large extent by the surface area of a metal target that is "looking at" the bottom of the searchcoil. You can prove for yourself that the actual volume or mass of a target has very little to do with most forms of detection.

With your detector operating move a large coin toward the searchcoil with the face of the coin "looking at" the bottom of the searchcoil. Note the distance at which the coin is detected. Now, move the coin back and rotate it so that the narrow edge "looks at" the searchcoil's bottom. Bring the coin in, and you will notice that it must come far closer to the searchcoil to be detected. The mass of metal itself did not change, only the surface area of the coin facing the searchcoil.

Another proof is to measure the distance a single coin can be detected. Then, stack several coins on the back side of the test coin and check to see how far this stack of coins can be detected. You'll find that the stack can be detected at only a slightly greater distance, illustrating that the greater volume of metal has very little effect on detection distance.

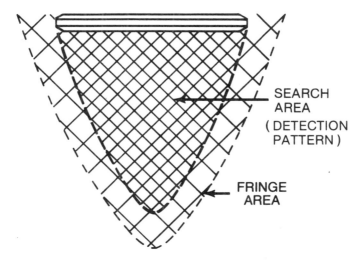

SEARCH AREA (DETECTION PATTERN)

FRINGE AREA

Targets can be located outside the normal detection pattern, but signals are too weak to be discerned except in the fringe area around the pattern's outer edges as illustrated here.

39

Fringe-area detection is a characteristic whose understanding will enable you to detect metal targets to the maximum depth capability of any instrument. The normal detection pattern for a coin may extend, say, nine inches below the searchcoil; the detection pattern for a small jar of coins may extend perhaps 18 inches below the searchcoil. Within these areas of detection an unmistakable detector signal is produced.

Does detection take place outside the detection pattern? *You bet!* Signals from this detection, however, are too weak to be heard by the operator except in the fringe area directly adjacent to the outer edges of the normal detection pattern.

If you want to hear fringe area signals, a good set of headphones is a must, along with training in the art of discerning those faint whispers of sound that can signal the presence of a coin in your fringe area. You can develop the ability to hear fringe area signals with practice, training, concentration and faith in your detector and its ability. Those of you who develop this fringe area detection capability will discover coins that other hobbyists miss. Combine your newfound capability with a modern instrument that can detect deeper and more precisely, and you have a coin hunting team that can't be beat!

Chapter 5
Coins & Things

The quantity of coins found by experienced coin hunters is in direct proportion to the amount of time and effort they spend in their search for coins. Earlier in this text I estimated that 5,000 coins per year is an easily attainable quantity for any hunter with even an average amount of success. A good coin hunter who remains active should find many more than that. And, even though the minimum face value of 5,000 coins might be only about $500 or less, the numismatic value of some of the older coins could cause the total value to soar.

Don't forget, too, that additional items of value will be found as well as coins. You'll discover these whether you're looking for them or not! Among these other metallic objects are such items as rings, jewelry, tokens, medallions and similarly valuable artifacts. The value of the gold and silver in jewelry will always remain high, and the market for artifacts and relics continues to grow even stronger.

In this book you will find pictures and stories of coin collections and other valuables amassed solely from the use of metal detectors by coin collectors. Neither the pictures nor the facts in the stories I share with you have been "faked" to try to induce people to take up the hobby of coin hunting or interest them in metal detecting. For, there is absolutely no need to fake; the facts speak for themselves!

The goal of this *Treasure Hunting Text* is to present the facts as we know them and to instruct, to the best of my capability, persons interested in the art of coin hunting. In Garrett and Ram files there are far more pictures of persons proudly displaying their coin finds than could be printed in a book many times the size of this one. And, some of these collections are truly small fortunes. I am constantly amazed at the quantity of wealth that today's coin and treasure hunters are recovering from the ground.

What They Find

In addition to coins the coin hunter finds rings, medallions, trade tokens, small metal toys, keys, tools (such as screwdrivers and pliers), caches of buried treasure and innumerable other items of value. To be rigorously honest, I must also report that the coin hunter also retrieves vast quantities of pulltabs, bits of non-ferrous metal, broken knives, spent cartridges, automobile parts, hinges, locks and I'll let each of you add his own *et cetera* to this list. The trash items just waiting to attract a metal detector are truly uncountable.

When Harry and Lucille Bowen of Spokane, WA, go coin hunting they wear aprons similar to one that a carpenter might wear. Their coin hunter's apron has two pockets – one for "good" items, the other for items "not so good." They store coins and other valuables in the "good" pocket and the junk items in the "not so good" pocket. I'll tell you later why they "keep" all this junk.

Occasionally the coin hunter will discover caches such as a jar filled with coins or other valuables. A coin hunter found 838 buffalo nickels buried in an old quart-sized fruit jar. Quite often "hot" money is found. It's ill-gotten cash which had been cached because nothing else could have been done with it at the time. Weapons such as guns, knives and swords are also found.

Objects Strange and Wonderful

It seems that each outing will turn up at least one peculiar thing. I once retrieved six 3-inch rusty steel washers from one

Above
This city park is a busy place in warm weather, but a coin hunter takes advantage of a pretty winter day to look for valuables lost by the summer crowds.
Below
A veteran Florida beach hunter found all of these coins in a single year of scanning the surfs and beaches with the right kind of metal detector.

hole. Apparently, someone never bothered to pick them up after they had finished their game of pitching washers. Virgil Hutton found three silver dollars in another hole, neatly stacked one on the other, at a city park in Austin, TX.

Chet Blanchard made the unusual discovery of a two-and-one-half-dollar gold piece inside an old iron dime bank. This occurred during a treasure hunting show when he left the exhibition building to try out a detector. He went searching around parking meters on the street looking for change that might have been dropped. Instead, his detector signalled an object that proved to be a rusty piece of iron. As he started to cast it aside, his eyes caught the glimmer of something shiny. He pried open the small rusty bank, and out fell the gold piece valued at many times its face value. One of the thrills of coin hunting is that you never know what wonderful thing your detector will discover next.

In this book you will occasionally find photos of objects other than coins that have been found by my treasure hunting companions and friends. I will also describe some of their valuable or unusual finds. The coin hunter who remains active quickly learns to expect the unreal.

I chuckle when I recall the story of a treasure hunter named Bob who was searching the ruins of an old town about 10 miles from Carthage in East Texas. In searching an old building for coins that might have become lodged in the cracks in its floor he received a strong signal over an area as large as a tub. He carefully removed several boards to find bare ground a few inches below. On probing in the dirt he struck wood and after about an hour's digging uncovered a box.

This box was filled with 50 ancient rifles and several handguns. They box was so deteriorated that it crumbled at a touch. All the weapons, however, had been carefully preserved with some sort of petroleum product. The guns were flintlocks and

Can you believe that Tom Edds of Merritt Island, FL, found all of these treasures . . . and they're just a part of the huge collection that he has amassed.

Check all finds carefully! Arvid Bergsten and Chet Blanchard inspect a $2.50 gold piece found in Downtown Houston in an old child's bank which Chet almost threw away as trash.

ball and cap rifles. On inquiry, the owner of the building reported that he knew nothing of the guns even though his family had owned the building for 90 years.

What a prize this turned out to be! Several of these old rifles are in the Garrett museum at our company's factory in Garland. Displayed along with these guns are hundreds of other items that coin and treasure hunters have found – guns, knives, swords, pistols, coins, jewelry, Civil War relics, farm implements and tools, Wells Fargo boxes and related items, Indian relics and many similar treasures.

Our museum is open to the public. If you are ever in the Dallas Metropolitan Area, drive out IH-635 to Garland and visit this museum at 2814 National Drive off Kingsley Road. It's free! And, it's always an enlightening experience to see the unusual items that other coin and treasure hunters have found.

Chapter 6

Where to Hunt

W here do successful coin hunters *find* all those coins? That's easy! They find them anywhere people have been – which is practically everywhere. Once a person has begun the fascinating hobby of coin hunting he will no longer need convincing that coins are waiting to be found. He will soon have the problem that other hobbyists face – simply too many places to search. When you begin finding coins, you will discover that the number of places to search is truly endless.

In this and the following chapter I have included a discussion and a list of the types of places where coins have been found, including some brief descriptions of exactly where to look for coins at that particular place. Now, my comments and my list are not meant to be all-inclusive. It never could be, for I'm adding new coin hunting locations to it daily, just as you will add them to your list.

People write to me telling about new discoveries. I read the newspaper and pick up valuable leads. I see bulletins from treasure hunting clubs and other publications written about coin hunters. Old friends and business associates share their secret places with me. I truly can hardly turn around without locating another new location just waiting to be searched for lost coins.

Oldtimers can tell you of places you could never learn about from other sources. Use your head; think! For instance, I searched for years before I suddenly realized that coin hunters should be able to find coins under a clothesline. And, sure enough, they were there. You can easily prove to yourself that even the neatest mothers and wives were unable to completely remove all the coins and metal objects from pockets of their children's and husbands' clothes before hanging them out to dry.

Gold Coins Waited

While on vacation with my family I struck up a conversation with a retired postman in a small north central Colorado town. He told me about a long-forgotten city park where a special event had once been held celebrating the founding of the city. Since gold had been instrumental to the growth of that old mining town, the city fathers decided to bury $5 gold pieces throughout the park for people to find. After a starter's pistol fired, townspeople could race through the park and scratch around looking for the coins. This "treasure hunt" would commemorate the city's founding.

Well, a good time was probably had by all, as they say. But, any detector operator could immediately see the value in searching this area! For some 70 years the gold coins that had gone undiscovered at the celebration just "slept" beneath the surface, waiting for the transmissions of a metal detector. There are many such areas throughout the United States.

Start at Home

Let me emphasize that you should never overlook the possibilities for finding coins at your very doorstep. Don't make the mistake of believing there are no coins to be found where you live. If you don't have the experience now, you soon will gain enough knowledge to convince yourself that coins are truly to be found everywhere. The first place every hobbyist should start searching is his own backyard.

I can't tell you how many people have complained to me that there is nothing in their area worth searching for. And, they're talking about their entire town or county! The truth is that it would take an army of thousands of coin hunters, working many years, to search and clean out all the productive areas existing today. And, by that time, think how many more additional coins would have been lost and would be waiting to be located!

Over the years I have heard many residents of the East Coast complain that metal detectors are useless in their area because there is nothing there to be found. The first time I heard this I could not understand how anyone could believe it until I began thinking. Yes, detectors had their beginning in the West where they were utilized primarily for prospecting . . . looking for nuggets and veins. Most of the instruments manufactured in the early years were produced on the West Coast. And, discoveries of precious metals are *still* made primarily in the West, with isolated exceptions in places such as Georgia.

As a result, residents of the East Coast generally think of metal detectors as being of value only in the search for precious metals; they "logically" conclude that detectors are useless in their particular areas. Of course, this is ridiculous!

The heavily populated East Coast of the United States is one of the world's hottest coin hunting areas. Since this section of the United States was settled first, it stands to reason that more old and, often, more valuable coins and artifacts have been lost there than anywhere else in the country. Since the area still contains the most dense clusters of people, there are greater numbers of coins and other precious objects being lost there every day.

In searching on the East Coast, the same basic rules given in this book apply. You will search the same kinds of places, using the same techniques for operating your detector. Rewards will be yours. Study your local history; talk to the old-timers; determine where old parks, meeting grounds, towns and communities were located. Where did people once congregate? Here, you will find your personal "hot spots." Here, you will find the old and valuable coins that make treasure hunting really pay off.

Coins, long ago hidden away and forgotten, await today's treasure hunters. These two small coin caches were discovered by Bill Mason of St. Paul, MN, who searches old farm houses.

About "Hot Spots"

You'll soon discover that so-called "hot spots" can be found in just about any given area. In other words, people have congregated in some places more than others. It's true today; it's always been so. You can learn about "hot spots" simply by observing people as they go about their daily routines. Drive over to your school or college campus. When you are at church, watch the people coming and going . . . see where they stand and talk, where their children run and play, where cars let out passengers. Just a little common sense and observation will enable you to increase your finds.

In a children's park or playground some of the better places to search are under swings, slides and gymnastic equipment. Naturally, children who turn head over heels are going to lose coins. Coins are commonly lost in picnic areas where people sit or lie down.

Your imagination will be called on when you investigate areas that are no longer used by the public. From your own experiences try to visualize where the crowds would have gathered. Then, develop "criss-cross" metal detection techniques that will let you sample the particular areas you have selected. As you search different areas, keep accurate count of the coins and jewelry you find and where you found them. From this data you will soon learn the probable location of the best places to search. Some hobbyists seem to be able just to walk into an old park and immediately begin scanning their detector over the exact spot where coins are to be found. Experience will enable you to become such a coin hunter!

Use Your Ears

Where were the old schools or meeting places located 50 or 100 years ago? At what locations did people gather in the past as they no longer do today? What about training camps, CCC camps, old reunion grounds, settlers' encampments, old communities that are now ghost towns? And, what about the ghost towns of yesterday that have totally disappeared today? The growing urbanization of America has caused many thriving rural communities to cease to exist completely . . . literally, to vanish from the face of the earth. Crops in the field grow silently where busy people congregated, transacted business and *lost coins!*

In your home town where are the long-forgotten fairgrounds, circus and carnival areas . . . the tent shows that were so popular in the days before air conditioning? What about the old swimming pools and picnic areas? Where were the old train, interurban and bus depots where so many commuters regularly removed coins and tokens from their pockets? There is no way that any single individual can know of all the rewarding coin hunting areas in a community.

Use your ears! Make it a habit to listen to the old-timers. Talk to family, friends, storekeepers – especially the older, retired people of the community who were postmen, bus drivers, merchants, policemen, firemen and the like. These individuals will have a wealth of information that can help you locate valuable coin hunting areas. And, don't ask them simply where you can find old coins. Just try to start them talking about the past . . . their activities and pleasures of yesterday.

What about nearby parks? How old are they? Are they in the same place now they were 50, 75 or 100 years ago? Check the

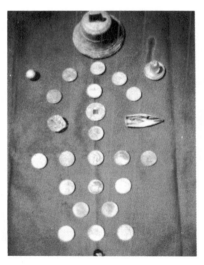 

These coins and other artifacts were recovered by San Diego treasure hunter George Mroczkowski and others searching the Old Town site. The single coin is a 1790 Venetian gold ducat.

official records of your city. Investigate vacant lots. What used to be there? As you drive through rural communities and small towns, stop to talk with the old-time residents. And, listen to them! You'll be amazed at how many are just waiting for an audience. Let them tell you where the general stores, saloons, banks and cafes used to be. Let them tell you of all the things that people used to do. That old-timer won't know it, but he'll be telling you where lost coins are waiting for your metal detector.

Personal Examples

Let me give you an idea of what I mean. About one-half mile from the little East Texas community of Pennington is the site of long-gone Steele Academy. This was a training school for boys that operated for many years before its doors closed long ago. This has proved to be a good coin hunting area.

From a museum curator in the historic town of Cripple Creek, CO, I found the location of an old picnic grounds, high above the city on a mountain top. This park and picnic area was once so popular that the local trolley car company built a track all the way to the park and had cars running continuously, especially on weekends. Think how many coins, 75 and 100 years old, lie here awaiting the avid coin hunter.

In my own area of Dallas I am familiar with parks that have been in use since before the turn of the century. Here, I have recovered numerous valuable coins. Surely, you know of similar parks in your areas.

One excellent method for finding the oldest coins is to locate geographically where your town or city was located when it was founded. Often, the present center of the town's activity is far removed from the original center of population. For example, the original town of San Diego, CA, is a few miles north of the present downtown area. When my family and I visited "Old Town" San Diego and talked with George Mroczkowski, he showed us where he had excavated at the site of old buildings to uncover many artifacts and valuable coins.

The Bill Wendels of Florida determined the location of the original site of Tampa, FL. Many relics and coins, including Spanish reales, half dimes, large cents and other denominations were found there. The American coins are dated in the 1830s. Even older coins could still be found because the original town of Tampa was erected just outside Fort Brooke's walls in 1823.

Older the Better

There is no doubt that most coin hunters truly enjoy getting out into the parks, playgrounds and other outdoor areas simply to search for lost coins and valuables. And, they delight at every discovery! But, let's face it – the finds that we enjoy *most* are those with the greatest value. This lets us benefit financially from the hobby. Thus, it behooves us to make the most diligent efforts to seek out and locate the coin hunting areas where the greatest number with the most value are to be found. Granted, each of us experiences a thrill when we dig up each coin, even when it is of current vintage and worth only face value.

But, I hope that each of you shares my special joy in finding something old . . . a remnant of the past. The half cents, large cents, two and three-cent pieces, half dimes, Liberty-seated quarters . . . and especially *gold* coins. These are often worth

Hobbyists using metal detectors assist professional historians to recover valuable artifacts from excavations at the location where Tampa, FL, was founded as Fort Brooke in the 1820's.

many times, often thousands of times, their face value . . . yet they provide an additional historical and romantic thrill. Such coins are seldom located in parks, around school yards or in areas of relatively recent occupancy. You must look for older habitations and areas of activity to find these older and rarer coins. This is where *research* pays off!

Your Research

Make it a daily habit to read the lost and found sections of newspapers, no matter where you find yourself. Quite often, persons losing valuables will advertise and post a reward for the return of their property. You can contact them and make prior agreements concerning your remuneration or reward if you can locate their lost valuables. Newspapers, too, are filled with information of the locations of public congregations (company picnics, family reunions and other such gatherings).

Spend time at the local library or newspaper office reviewing the issues of yesteryear. You will learn the location of old parks and playgrounds, band concert sites, fairground and circus lots, along with information on public activities that occurred in the past. Notices of lost articles can also be found here. Only your enthusiasm will limit your efforts and your success. And . . . if you are a dedicated treasure hunter, you will discover many heart-fluttering stories that suggest veritable bonanzas. May you find some of them!

Bulletin boards in laundromats or stores and other public areas often contain notices of lost items. It will pay you to check these places frequently. Why not post your own "Have Detector . . . Will Travel!" notices on these free bulletin boards?

It's a good idea to make contact with local police and insurance agents or even insurers and law enforcement officials outside your area. Tell them you have a metal detector and that you are willing to help them locate lost jewelry and other valuables. You may be surprised at the services you can perform, as well as the rewards you will receive. This is just another example of how the owner of a metal detector can increase his annual income with only a reasonable amount of thought and physical effort.

It's Up to You

There is no way that I can stress strongly enough the importance of ideas presented in this and the following chapters. Sure, coins are just waiting to found nearly everywhere, and I know that each of you will find a goodly number of them. Still, the maximum monetary value in coin hunting and the greatest personal rewards come from finding the old, valuable coins . . . and, finding them as a result of your own research, investigation and hard work. True, you'll probably never actually grow tired of recent coins . . . no matter how many of them you find in parks and playgrounds. But, you'll get so much more pleasure and vastly larger rewards from recovering old and rare coins in places you have discovered through your own desire and careful investigative efforts. You can only grow even more enthusiastic as your rewards increase!

In this chapter I have tried to stir your imagination about the great potential of coin hunting . . . to help you understand how coins can be found *everywhere.* I hope that you will understand, however, that some effort is required if you are to receive any benefits from coin hunting . . . and, that *much* effort will be necessary to achieve the maximum benefits. Research, planning

While on an automobile trip in the Pacific Northwest, the author, Roy Lagal and Frank Duvall broke the monotony of their drive by stopping to search this roadside park for coins.

and a great deal of investigative work and thought will be necessary.

The following chapter will include as many places as I know of or have been told about where coins have actually been found. I have also included lists of the sorts of people you should seek out and listen to. Throughout this book, you will find scattered bits of information designed to help your research . . . to aid you in seeking out and locating additional sites for coin hunting. I can't repeat enough the simple truism that your success depends entirely upon your effort. The coins are there; it's up to you to find them!

Chapter 7

Places & People

Here are some general ideas about where you can find coins with a metal detector. The list is by no means all-inclusive, nor will it *ever* be complete . . .

PLACES WHERE PEOPLE HAVE LIVED

Inside

Closets and shelves – single coins could lie unnoticed on old shelving. Look behind shelving on the braces supporting shelves.

In the walls.

Above and beneath door and window sills; in the doors. (I know of a $50 gold piece worth several thousand dollars that was found between the window and sill in an old house.)

Underneath or along baseboards and quarter-rounds.

Underneath and along edges of linoleum or other flooring, particularly beneath or inside layers of floor covering and near holes in the covering.

Old garages.

Basements, sheds, barns, haylofts and other outbuildings, such as chicken houses, stables and other animal shelters.

Crawl spaces under houses and other buildings.

Outside

Your own yards, front as well as back.

Driveways, especially where passengers or drivers would have normally gotten out of cars, carriages or wagons.

Front doors; people reaching into pockets for keys might have dropped coins.

Under houses, porches and steps, especially those with hand-rails where children might have played and rolled coins through.

Around and along all walks and paths.

Around old outhouses; coins often fell out while clothing was being "adjusted;" look all around on the ground where the outhouses used to stand and along trails that led from them to the main house.

Around hitching posts and hitching post racks.

Between gate posts.

Around mail boxes, both rural and urban; many a coin left in olden days to pay for postage now lies buried in the dirt.

Well and pump sites.

Storm cellar and basement steps.

Around old watering troughs.

Along fence rows, especially around stiles, gates or other breaks in the fences.

Under trees, especially where "shade-tree mechanics" might have worked on automobiles. Children play under trees and swing on them as well. I remember children playing and swinging on trees in my old neighborhood; I'm sure they lost coins that are still waiting to be found.

Under clotheslines or places where they once stood, as well as along fences in rural areas where clothes might have been hung to dry.

In back yards and around garden furniture areas; look for permanently installed benches around trees or permanent rest areas such as gazebos.

Areas where children may have had refreshment stands

PLACES WHERE PEOPLE HAVE BEEN

Recreation and Camping Areas

Fishing piers, boat ramps and landings.

Back-country fishing camps and health resorts.

Resort areas of any kind.

Horse and hiking trails where riders or backpackers might have normally stopped or camped.

Swimming areas, especially those without bathhouse or other facilities.

Children's camps (even active ones, during the off season); be especially watchful around concession areas, cabin or tent sites and recreational areas where games might have been played.

At loading and unloading areas of ski tows.

Swimming beaches; at low tide get out into the water as deeply as you can submerge your searchcoil.

Miniature golf courses and driving ranges.

Rifle and pistol shooting ranges – expect to find lots of shell casings but coins as well.

Bluffs and embankments where children might have slid on real or improvised sleds.

Under the grandstand seats in stadiums of all kinds and sizes.

Around bandstands, gazebos, dance floors and other entertainment platforms where people once congregated.

Amusement parks and fairgrounds, carnival and circus sites, particularly where coin pitches and midway "action" games could have been played (watches or rings could have slipped off); around concession stand locations and ticket booths; under rides which might have jostled valuables loose.

Rodeo grounds or old horse race tracks, especially where betting occurred.

At motor speedways around ramps for cars or cycles.

Parks – around benches and drinking fountains; under trees and around steps; under swings, slides and exercise equipment; around little hills and valleys which might have attracted activity; around and under picnic tables; football and baseball playing areas.

Drive-in theaters – up front around children's playground equipment; around speaker poles; concession stand areas;

These two trees stand at what was once the doorway of a church in Maryland that was torn down long ago. Coins and other valuables lost here still await THers with metal detectors.

around the protected area in front of the projection booth; around ticket windows.

Along Their Travels

At ferryboat loading and unloading areas.

Any old springs where wagon trains or settlers might have camped. (Many of these old springs served as "wishing wells" and should be investigated.)

River fords; look in the shallows of both sides as well as on the banks. Check for nearby camping areas; valuables cached here might never have been recovered.

Trailer park areas – not only are these good locations because people have lived here, but there has been considerable movement. Some trailer areas have been struck by windstorms which overturned trailers, spilling valuables which may not all have been recovered.

Motels and tourist courts, especially around recreational areas, vending machines, concession areas and swimming pools.

Historical markers, highway monuments or other areas that are popular photographic stops.

Tourist stops of any kind, such as wishing wells and wishing bridges, hilltops overlooking large expanses of scenery, mountain passes, scenic overlooks along parkways and canyons. Remember to look below such lookouts or under bridges or towers where people might have tossed coins for luck or where rings and watches might have fallen.

Along highways near litter cans. When throwing trash from

Above
Not particularly old or of much value beyond their denomination . . . still, imagine what a prize these were to the detector hobbyist who found them!
Below
The spectators have left, but whatever they lost at the game remains behind. The area beneath any stadium seats is a prime target for coin hunters.

cars, people occasionally lose rings, bracelets and other valuables. Children (of all ages) have also been known to throw valuables from cars.

In roadside parks and at tourist stops, especially along footpaths or in shady areas where people might have rested.

Stagecoach stops and relay stations, especially those which supported trading posts.

Old shipping pen areas for livestock.

Abandoned railroad depots.

Trolley and bus stops, commercial lines as well as the areas where children boarded school buses.

Wherever They Might Have Congregated

Around service stations, particularly the older ones.

In church yards, where members might have stood around in conversation before or after services; around trees where children played; around any steps, walks and in passenger unloading areas; where tables were built for meals.

Rural church revival areas, especially those featuring "dinner on the ground."

Brush arbors. (If you don't know what they are, read on to learn...and enhance your understanding of Americana.)

Cemeteries.

Schools and colleges—around playground equipment, bicycle racks, outside cafeteria doors where lines formed, at water fountains or wells, shaded walk or rest areas. Stop by active schools while classes are in session and check to see where students and teachers congregate.

Highway cafes and truck stops.

Roadside stands, where items such as fruit, vegetables and fireworks have been sold. Money changed hands often; some coins must have been lost.

Beaches where crowds might once have gathered for enter-

Research led this coin hunter to an old Army barracks where 50-year-old coins were waiting for his modern computerized detector.

63

tainment or to witness such events as a sinking ship or other disaster.

Around beach furniture.

At the ocean's edge, especially after a hurricane or other storm.

At any area where a disaster has occurred – fire, flood, earthquake, etc.

After any fire, around burned buildings and houses. Here, it is quite common to find clumps of coins that were melted together by the heat.

At the site of train, auto or airplane wrecks; especially look for jewelry.

Locations where an old building has recently been razed; you'll locate lots of metal fragments, but coins and valuables as well.

Areas where bulldozers have engaged in earth-moving. Deeply buried caches are sometimes found in such areas when they have been exposed. Old-timers can help here with their stories. And, don't forget, when bulldozers remove topsoil they get you closer to *all* the treasures beneath it!

Underneath any boardwalks.

Ghost towns – along the boardwalks, in the streets, in stores and commercial areas.

Around fire escapes permanently attached to buildings. (I remember, as a lad, sliding down a fire escape from the second floor of a church many times.)

Graveled parking lots at any business or recreational area.

Anywhere else where cars have been parked. Around parking meters and along grassy strips where cars might park; parking lots, especially along fences into which paper money could have blown; in grassy areas adjacent to the parking lots of malls.

At car washes or the water/air areas adjacent to service stations. Look on top of the coin box where people sometimes place coins, then forget them when they are not needed.

Around drive-in grocery stores, especially sides and backs where groups might have congregated.

Telephone booths.

Old bars, taverns and inns. Don't forget beer gardens . . . those with a few inches of loose gravel can be especially rewarding.

Construction sites—watch for areas where catering trucks sell food and drink to workers.

Fireplugs. (Dogs don't lose coins here, but children do when they play games leaping over them.)

Nursing home lawns and walks, around seating areas.

Flea markets and auctions; lots where they are held; parking lots for their customers.

Courthouses and other government and public buildings; lawns, walkways and areas where people might have lain or rested.

Caves. Caution: caves may produce more "bats" than bucks!

PEOPLE TO LISTEN TO

Policemen can tell you where items of value might have been lost; you can often earn a reward by helping them recover these items.

Insurance agents are often glad to tip you off to help them locate lost valuables.

What stories this old bench could tell! And, don't you imagine that during its decades of service, it might have witnessed the loss of a coin or two . . . just waiting now to be recovered.

Highway clean-up crews usually know locations where coins and valuables have been found. This can occur at waste disposal areas and at exits from tourist stops.

Lifeguards at swimming areas can often point out specific sites where valuable jewelry has been lost.

Jewelry store personnel sometimes hear stories about lost valuables that customers have replaced.

Pawn shop personnel can give you similar information.

Old-timers and retired individuals can provide your waybills to treasure. Just let them talk and pay close attention.

Firemen can help you locate burned houses and stores that were never rebuilt.

Ministers, priests and rabbis may be able to guide you to long forgotten areas where worship services were once held. .

Historians and archaeologists can sometimes provide the location of once-populated but now deserted and forgotten community sites. Suggestion: don't try to debate the ethics of metal detectors with professionals in this field; many of them have warped ideas about hobbyists and treasure hunters generally.

Railroad engineers and conductors (especially those who are retired) might know the location of old and forgotten railroad depots and loading areas that are no longer used.

Park supervisory personnel can help you determine where people now congregate as well as the possible locations of former bandstands, picnic tables, slides, swings and other playground equipment.

Bus drivers (here, again, look for retirees) sometimes know of long forgotten communities they once served.

READ ABOUT THEM

"Listen" to history books written about the areas you are interested in exploring. Read all the books you can on local history. No matter what you *think* you know about an area, seek all the information you can obtain from others. With each history book – amateur or professional – that you read, you will arm yourself with additional knowledge of dozens of places that can possibly yield large quantities of old and valuable coins.

Most newcomers to the hobby think that research is dull work; they'd rather "get into action" by scanning (often haphazardly) with a metal detector. Usually, they are simply wasting

Containing Mexican coins and currency, this cache recovered
by Frank Angona proved to be not particularly valuable, but he
said that his thrill of discovery made the find worthwhile.

time because they are dead wrong about research.

It's sometimes hard work, but it pays off! Research is profitable in many different ways, and to me it is as much fun as the actual treasure hunt itself. Many people tell me, "Oh, I have so little time for the hobby; I don't want to waste any on research." Actually, the right kind of research helps you *save* time and can greatly increase the value of your take.

Spend time at your libraries or newspaper offices reviewing newspapers of yesteryear. Believe me; you won't have nearly enough time to search out all possibilities you uncover there! Visit museums and study maps for locations of old communities that will provide good coin hunting sites today. Watch newspaper "Lost and Found" sections for possibilities.

Chapter 8

In the City

As you can probably imagine, most coin hunting takes place in cities or, at least, in good-sized towns. It is here that the most people congregate. And, the place to find lost coins is where people have lost them!

A complete list of places to hunt for coins in a modern community would be truly unending. In this chapter I will discuss the areas that are more frequently searched . . . those areas that have most often proved productive for me and many of the coin hunters with whom I associate. From my own experiences and those of my friends I'll also offer a few ideas and hints that might help you in your own search for coins.

Of course, wherever people walk they lose coins. Search along all sidewalks. Be especially thorough at intersections or corners where people stop to wait for traffic. Grassy areas at intersections always yield a few coins or tokens. Check around benches at bus stops; if there are no benches remaining, try to visualize where they might have been.

Old homes are an ideal city place to find coins of all ages. The most likely places for finding them with a metal detector are around front porches and walks; in driveways where people got in and out of cars, buggies and wagons; around hitching posts; around back door steps; along any walk areas; under clotheslines; under and around trees where children might have played, built treehouses or swung from limbs or ropes suspended from them.

Be very careful in your search of all old garages or carriage houses. These areas often served a far more diverse function in past years. Storing the family's automobile(s) or other means of transportation was but one of the uses for this section of the homestead. It was often a popular meeting place, especially for boys and children.

Coins have been found in various places literally all over the inside of old houses. Such places would include closet shelves where a single coin could lie unnoticed on the shelf itself or back behind where it fell or was hidden. I always hope that the coins that I find have been "hidden" rather than just "lost" because people are more prone to hide valuables! A detector (hand-held, perhaps) can often detect coins between the walls, especially where a child could push them through tiny cracks; under rugs and carpets; in cracks in the floor; between the floor and the baseboards or quarter-rounds; inside doors and their locks.

No matter what type of floor coverings are used in a house, scan over them carefully . . . especially around holes or at the edges. I've seen instances where individual coins were tucked under vinyl or stuffed under the carpet or between it and the mat. Apparently the coins were placed there by young children. In addition to children who push and hide coins under holes and edges of floor coverings, coins could also have been swept accidentally into such places during vigorous house-cleaning. A. T. Evans of Eureka Press and "Father" of the *Treasure Hunters Yearbooks* indicated that some very nice individual coins have been found between the baseboards and the floor, apparently swept underneath as the room was cleaned. Additionally, look for coins under the doorsills where they may have been swept or pushed.

Bless the Children!

On first thought, you might say to yourself, "Who cares about the coins lost by children! They were probably just pennies, or nickels . . . dimes at most."

Let me answer you with a question, "Do you like to find Indianhead pennies? How about some Barber dimes?"

Don't scoff at the lost coins of children. They can make you wealthy. To find these "leavings," however, it helps if you can think as a child. Remember, when you were one? Where did you hide coins? As you search old houses, look around the rooms and try to think as a child would. Even stoop over to place your head on the level of a child's. Look around the room and observe places where coins could be squirreled away . . . where they could be hidden quickly. Some coins have been found in door locks. Any type of lock with a keyhole large enough for a dime or penny is a good place to search, even though you may have to dismantle the lock to recover your find, When you do this, make certain you replace the lock as it was . . . unless you own the house.

When I heard this story from an old friend, I thought about children. He told me of searching an old house relentlessly and finding mostly junk and only a few coins. As he left, however, his searchcoil brushed against the wooden front door. Luckily, he had neglected to turn his detector off, for it responded to the door with a loud squeal. He admits being lucky, but he found a cache of coins that apparently had been dropped, one at a time, down into this hollow door through a small crack in it.

More Luck

A similar incident occurred when a carpenter was engaged to replace several rotting boards on the outside of a big, old, wooden house. As he began pulling off the rotten boards, half-dollars poured out of the wall onto the ground. Several hundred old Liberty-walking half-dollars were recovered. Nobody knows how the coins got there, but it was known that some 30 years

Roy Lagal, left, and Tommy T. Long use early VLF detectors to find coins left behind by the old BFOs. Tomorrow's instruments will locate treasures being overlooked today!

earlier the structure had served as a house of ill repute. Tip money, maybe?

When searching old houses, always look for the early style electrical fuse boxes. (Remember when people substituted pennies for burnt-out fuses?) I can recall my grandmother *replacing* fuses with pennies every time she ironed. Apparently her iron drew more current than the fuse capability, and she needed to beef up the current supply by letting the penny serve as a fuse. When you find these old fuse boxes, look into the box to make certain there are no dirt-covered coins. Also, look on top and around it where people might have placed coins for emergency use. *Caution:* always make certain that fuse boxes are disconnected from the power supply before you attempt to search them by hand.

Ever hear of the old superstition of placing "good luck" coins around the foundation piers of houses and other buildings? It may sound like mumbo-jumbo, but it's something we coin hunters can capitalize on. Always search around the corners of old houses, especially around sites where houses have been torn down. A. T. Evans points out that you can still find the ruins of old courthouses in abandoned towns. "Find the cornerstone," he urges, "and you are likely to reap a real treasure in both money and historical items." He calls attention to the custom (often, still followed) of placing various items and paraphernalia inside cornerstones when dedicating or breaking ground for a structure. Of course, it's always a good idea to share with the local historical society or museum any noticeable finds you make.

Through the Floor

Another good story from fellow treasure hunter Evans: In Big Spring, TX, a coin hunter chanced to overhear an elderly gentleman tell how, when a small boy, he and friends used to snitch coins from his father's cash drawer while he was busy barbering. They would then drop them through cracks in the floor to be recovered later. Investigation by the coin hunters showed the old house still to be in the same location. Wonder of wonders, it was built on stilts with the floor about three feet off the ground, leaving plenty of room to crawl underneath with a detector.

More than 200 old coins were found here. Needless to say, the lads were better at snitching than recovering the fruits of their thievery!

Perhaps you laughed when you saw "outhouses" listed in the previous chapter as a likely searching place. Well, you shouldn't have! These seem to be excellent places to find old coins, especially if the hobbyist can search the ground on which the old building actually stood. Apparently many coins fell from men's and boys' trousers, dropped between cracks in the floor and were gradually covered by dirt. Search the trail that leads

Coins are lost where people have been. Think of the countless men, women and children over the years who have walked along the streets and sidewalks of America's towns and cities!

between the house and the outhouse. Sometimes people seemed to be in quite a hurry to get out to the Montgomery Ward catalog!

If you're interested in relic and bottle hunting, consider digging old outhouse pits. This may not sound attractive, but I'm assured by experts that body wastes decompose quite rapidly and are not harmful at all after only a few years. Ask your doctor! Anyway, these pits are a favorite digging place for dedicated bottle hunters who tell me about small fortunes that have been taken from pits in the form of bottles, guns, coins and other relics. Seems that when a pit was abandoned, it was often used as a dump for discarded items.

Parks and Playgrounds

You'll find playgrounds high on anyone's list of where coins are to be found in large quantities, but your coins here will probably be recent ones. Therefore, they will be of little value beyond their face denomination. But, since any "sound of money" from your Garrett detector makes sweet music to your ears, a visit to the nearest playground may be a sure way to get out of the dumps and cure your blues. Rarely will you be disappointed here!

If the above statements don't ring true, I challenge you to visit any playground. Watch the children and young people while they play. See them run and fall; look at them tumble about, head over heels, on various pieces of equipment. It will pay you to search carefully near each and every playground apparatus. Careful coin hunters will usually get a few worthwhile signals around the see-saws, swings, tumble bars and other places for climbing and playing.

The athletic fields at many playgrounds can be equally fruitful in their production of coins. Don't forget the stands where spectators observe the youth at play. If there is a swimming pool, search the grassy areas around it where parents and friends watch the swimmers. Look around all drinking fountains, picnic tables and benches. Pay attention to children at play; see where their activities lead them. Here, coins certainly await your detector.

Make a concerted effort to search parks and playgrounds as they *used to be*. I recall seeing a very old map of New York's Central Park printed alongside a modern map to illustrate the park's development. The old map showed locations of bandstands, concession stands and other crowd-drawing attractions no longer in existence. Such sites could prove very rewarding.

George Sullivan, author of *Do-It-Yourself Moving*, tells of a man who has recovered 30,000 coins from New York state parks. Coins are being lost by the "pants-pocket-full" at parks all around you . . . every day. Don't miss the fun of recovering them!

Lakes are often found in conjunction with parks, but there may not be any "playgrounds," as such, designated around them. Still, lakes are attractive to the coin hunter for a number of reasons, and I urge you to review all of these as they apply in areas where you hunt.

For example, from time to time lakes are dredged in order to deepen them and enhance their value. Sometimes this is done simply to dispose of the silt that has accumulated. Regardless, when you hear of this occurring, try to locate the area where the dump dirt is being taken. It may be directly adjacent to the lake. Scan this material for artifacts and other valuables. The bottoms of most lakes contain many lost items and others discarded on purpose. Among these are guns, knives, fishing tackle, jewelry, coins and relics. The dump site might give you the chance to recover some of these.

During the drouth of the summer of 1988 water receded to such an extent at a lake in Idaho that the original townsite of American Falls was exposed. Members of the Gate City Treasure Hunters Club of Pocatello reported some remarkable finds.

Also to be found in many parks are wishing wells, ponds, streams and similar areas where coins are traditionally tossed. Of course, such areas are usually protected from the public and probably cleaned out on a regular basis. If you are lucky, however, you might find one that is located near or beneath a grassy area where people stand to throw their coins. Here, you might find some coins that have been accidentally dropped. Children especially are quite good at dropping coins they intend to toss into the well.

Many times old community playgrounds and other gathering places were the location for public cisterns or wells. People would come here to draw a bucket of drinking water. Often coins were tossed in the well for luck. Perhaps some were lost on the ground in the process. In addition, such wells and cisterns often featured overhead coverings which offered protection on hot or rainy days. People would congregate, sit down and – you guessed it – lose coins.

Bleachers and Grandstands

Rarely will you ever fail to find coins under and around stadium seats. This is just as true at the children's ball park as it is at a major league arena. And, it's far more likely you'll have the opportunity to search the kids' parks!

In addition to coins you will find watches, rings, knives, keys and many other objects that have fallen through the stands. Spectators become quite excited at times and, without knowing it, supply us treasure hunters with loot galore! Depending on the size of the crowd that used the stadiums, such areas below bleachers can become quite cluttered with cans, bottles, cigarette packages, gum wrappers and other bits of junk. Carry along a rake and perhaps even a weed-cutter to clean the areas for easier searching. Always be on the alert here for paper money; occasionally you will find some.

Don't forget the fences around stadium seating areas. Here is where you will often find paper money that has been blown by the wind. The same theory holds true for any wire fence that the wind can blow through. Let me tell you about a large shopping center near my home. Its parking lot must cover some ten acres or more. All along the north and west sides of this paved lot is a chain-link fence. Since prevailing summer winds here blow from the south and southeast, lots of papers and other light trash are regularly blown against this fence where it all accumulates in profusion.

One day when I was leaving the lot, I spied a dollar bill being whisked through the air by the wind. Finally, it came to rest among the trash that had also blown into the fence, and it turned out to be a $5 bill. There must be dozens of fenced areas such as this in any town or city of even moderate size. Here, of course, you don't need a metal detector. In addition to money, who knows what else of value (or interest) you might find.

Speaking of parking areas, as we were in the preceding paragraph, these seem to be locations where people are always losing coins as they get out of cars or remove keys from their pocket to unlock a car. Most big parking lots are paved nowadays, but there are still plenty of places were people park on gravel. Here, your metal detector can find those coins that were dropped.

More on parking . . . don't forget the grassy areas where parking meters are located. Because these are highly public areas, you'll always want to be especially neat in your probing and digging.

Fairs and Circuses

Almost all towns and cities at one time or another had an area designated for the fairgrounds. In my home town of Lufkin, TX, I attended a fair every year at the same location when I was growing up. My parents told me that the same fairgrounds had been used for some 20 years prior to that. And, before then, the fairgrounds had been located at another site.

Such areas are almost always excellent places to search. You must be especially thorough here because most coins – at least the older and more valuable ones – are buried deeply. It's quite common to find them very deep. If you can find an old-timer, ask him where the concessions, the midway and the coin-pitch tents were located. These will really be "hot spots" for you to search.

Concession stands and ticket booths were generally located in all areas where people congregated either to entertain themselves or to be entertained. Make special effort to search both inside and outside such stands. Also search quite a way out from of the concession stands and ticket booths for the possible coins people dropped while walking away with an armful of popcorn, peanuts or hot dogs.

In addition to coins, you may find tokens here if the location of your booths is ancient enough. In the past patrons were sometimes issued tokens which could be redeemed at ticket windows for later events. Such tokens are of real value to some collectors. Don't overlook or discard them!

In the days before air conditioning there were a number of circuses of all sizes that performed "under the big top" outdoors. Even the smallest towns seemed to attract one of these tent shows occasionally. They would set themselves up for a day or so on a convenient vacant lot or parking lot. Many coins were lost here as adults and children attended the circus and did all the things that you and I have done at one of them. When you find one of these old areas, you'll probably have your greatest success at their midway locations . . . just as you did at old fairgrounds. You may be even lucker here because you might find yourself exploring an area that has never been searched before!

I know of one hobbyist who discovered an old publication that listed pre-1900 fairground sites all over the United States. What a bonanza in old coins he reaped at these locations! And, because he found most of them to be plowed fields or grazing lands at the time he searched, he had little difficulty with scanning and digging.

Perhaps you can locate lists such as his or those for other such locations from historical societies or similar groups. Look for old city and state parks, settlers' reunion grounds, circus locations, race tracks, revival meeting places. Such a list could go on endlessly. You can probably add more examples yourself!

Schools

Some hobbyists scoff at searching around schoolyards. "Children's pennies," they sneer. Please don't be one of these. I have been successful in finding coins of all denominations – and, all *ages* – on the grounds of schools and colleges. Almost all areas around them will be productive. Search first around sidewalks, trees and playground equipment.

Let your imagination be your guide. Better yet, if you are able

The old and new meet as Charles Garrett examines an ancient Roman coin he has just discovered in a field in England with a modern metal detector.

to observe children while they are in school, you can go well prepared at the earliest opportunity to search the areas where coins are most likely to be found. I recall when I was a student at Kurth Elementary School in Lufkin, we would march over to the high school at lunchtime and form a line outside the door . . . the area was grass, and I know that coins were lost here. I lost some myself! Recently, I returned to search the area and, guess what? The site was a paved parking lot. The moral to that story: *don't procrastinate!* When you discover or remember a potentially good site, *go . . . then!*

College campuses are productive sites. No matter how old or smart we are, we still lose money. College students are no exception. These young men and women sit and lie on the campus grass more than high school students because they usually have more time between classes. They sit or lie down to rest, eat, talk, study – and lose coins and other items of value.

Like college students people going to church lose coins too. Not all those destined for the collection plate make it there! Some of these coins find their way into the dirt and grass outside the church doors or on its parking lots. Always check churches wherever you search.

Grassy areas along walks and around steps are generally good producers. Likewise, always search areas where cars might pull in to unload passengers, especially when these places are either obvious or so designated. If the ground here is not paved, you can expect to find coins that latecomers lose as they leap from their cars, or coins that fall from hands large and small as individuals dressed in their Sunday best try to hold onto Bibles, handbags, umbrellas, walking sticks and you-name-it.

Reading Newspapers

Wherever you find yourself, always read the local news-

Minerals in the clay of old chimney bricks present no problems to a modern metal detector which has circuitry that can be precisely ground balanced.

paper(s) with the idea of coin hunting in mind. This is true of the large daily newspapers in the big cities or the small weeklies in the country. Be imaginative in your thinking. Always visualize were coins might be found.

Newspapers will often point out to you areas of either construction or destruction, both accidental and intentional. Quite often during excavation work or house-wrecking activities, coins can be found rather easily. They will be in the walls of old houses and beneath the piers and foundations. Frequently, bulldozers and other earth-moving equipment will dig up caches of coins, and this happening will be publicized in the newspapers. Find out where these places are and go out with your metal detector. Oftentimes, you can find coins and valuables just lying around the site.

As you become more proficient in your habit of scanning newspapers, never overlook the "lost and found" columns. Many people who lose valuable jewelry offer rewards which provide golden opportunities for you. Also, try to arrange for your "good deed" of recovering a lost valuable to be reported in the newspaper where it will serve as an advertisement for your services. How many people know just *exactly* where they lost that ring, watch, earring or other valuable? But, they've never thought of using a metal detector to recover it. You can help them . . . for profit!

When reading the newspapers, watch for announcements of the locations of outdoor parties and gatherings. Knowledge of these spots could be valuable to you as a coin hunter.

In cities and towns all over the country various groups meet on a regular basis for celebrations and festivals. I always recall a story of one of these which was brought to my attention by Ed Batholomew of Fort Davis, TX.

In a small gold-mining town in the West was a large group of people of German descent. Once a year they met at a certain rather isolated crossroads location for a day-long get-together which included all sorts of dancing, playing and other festivities. Ed tells me that the beer and Rhine wine flowed freely throughout the day, and by late afternoon spirits were quite high – and, sometimes, tempers as well. Consequently, without fail, the men began brawling – in a friendly manner, of course – and a great deal of fighting and wrestling took place. The amount of coins lost by these men is reported to be astronomical. The annual events have not been held for many years; the isolated area has been worked time and again by coin hunters. Yet, more coins are still being found there . . . and, they are growing older by the day!

Coins in the Straw

Another story I heard about recently came from a farm town in the Plains states. During some sort of annual festivity each year a special event was held just for the town's children. Into a huge haystack handfuls of coins were tossed, and the boys and girls leaped into the hay to scramble around, jostle each other and generally have a great time recovering coins to their hearts' content. This event was staged over and over again for many years. Naturally, when a coin hunter heard about it, he kept inquiring of old-timers until he found the spots where the haystacks had been located.

Yep! You guessed the rest. His trusty Garrett discovered

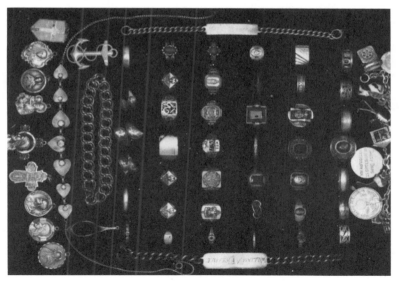

When your detector signals, you never know what it's found! Coin hunters recover all sorts of unusual objects such as those shown here in this collection of an Oregon treasure hunter.

83

more coins for him that you could ever believe. Those farm kids just thought they found them all! And, you know what? I bet there are still coins there to be found.

My parents once operated a furniture store in an old building whose rear section was utilized as a storage area. Portions of the floor had been torn out. One day when I was working back there, I found a silver dollar-sized token in the dirt, and asked my father about it. He recalled that the building had once housed an illegal gambling casino. Sure enough, the long arm of the law finally reached in and destroyed all the gaming equipment. The casino was finished, but literally hundreds of metal tokens for slot machines and other gambling purposes were lost in the dirt beneath the floor. Believe me, I spent many days "getting rich" (and plenty dirty) on the floor of that old store.

All these stories were designed to stir the memories of some of you . . . to help you recall similar locations where you can locate "hot spots." I know that such spots exist (though, certainly not as old casinos) all over the country. You'll just have to "dust off" your memory and recollect them.

Have you begun thinking about unusual sites where you can

Colorado THer Glenn Carson found all of these items around old footings at Delagua, a coal camp south of Walsenburg. He searches for coins at active and abandoned mining areas.

hunt coins? Perhaps there are some that *only you* know about. I hope so! There are many, many coin hunting areas that can be found in cities and towns . . . many more in addition to those listed in these and the other chapters of this book. Use your imagination and then follow the sound of your detector to happiness and wealth!

Chapter 9

In the Country

Whentraveling, it is always a good idea to leave early to allow extra time for coin hunting in the country through which you will pass. There are many places all along roads and highways that can prove very profitable. You don't necessarily have to get far off the major arteries to locate them either! The last time that I drove from Dallas to Odessa on Interstate 20 I counted at least a half-dozen drive-in theaters, most of them deserted and in varying stages of disrepair. At these old outdoor "picture shows" are many, many coins waiting for you, and some of them could have numismatic value equivalent to the cost of a good new detector.

Abandoned stores and cafes along the highway, roadside parks, camping, hunting and fishing grounds can be found alongside roads no matter where you travel. Stops such as these can prove doubly profitable as you give yourself and your family a chance to stretch their legs . . . or walk the dog!

Where Children Play

If you have children, watch where they play when you stop at a roadside park or rest stop. If children no longer accompany you on travels, watch those with other people and try to recollect how your own once acted. The point I'm trying to make is that you can find coins in areas where children play. Locate them!

One type of place that should always be searched is any hill or small cliff in playgrounds and parks. Young people seem to be drawn, as if by a magnet, to a spot where they can jump out into the air, run back up and jump off again. I can recall that when my children used to travel with us through the mountains, they would always seek out the little hills for playing whenever we would stop. I'm certain they lost coins many times.

In your hometown or other places with which you are familiar, look for ramps and hills where motorcyclists have tried out their skills. You know what I mean . . . they race up the hill to soar over it, raising the front of their bike to "pop wheelies." Also, you may remember areas where you, as a young person, used to slide down an embankment . . . either in cardboard boxes or on a snow sled. These places where people have been active are always good for coins, knives and other items normally carried in the pocket.

If there's a big cardboard box at hand, why not try out the slide yourself? See if you're still good at it . . . see how young you really are! After all, metal detectors are really adult toys, like guns, golf clubs, skis, bows and arrows and the like. If you think you're too old for childish endeavors, what are you doing with a metal detector?

The Back Roads

Of course, the farther off the beaten path your travels take you, the more likely you are to find old settlements and places where coin hunting can be particularly good. Why not check the map before you head out on your next driving trip? Look for alternate routes that let you get there by taking back roads. Instead of crowding the speed limit and worrying about a traffic ticket, you can drive comfortably and relaxed. You'll appreciate the scenery for a change, and you'll also enjoy the coins that you find at such places as old courthouses and community recreational areas in some of the small, off-the-Interstate locations.

Of course, you'll need leads. Without these, your scanning will bring you little more than fresh air, sunshine or exercise. Of course, that's quite a bit in itself!

The best way to get leads is to talk with people who are familiar with the little towns through which you travel . . . the residents and old-timers who can direct you to the parks, old campgrounds, peddler's stands, fairgrounds and similar places. There always seem to be some of these older men and women sitting on benches in parks, along the town's streets or in the stores and cafes.

My friend Fred Mott of Dallas suggests that you approach these folks (especially if they are obviously senior citizens) by asking them if they "know where you can find any real old-timers." Of course, this generally gets a laugh and makes them feel good while identifying you as a decent sort of person. Once the ice is broken and they've identified you as sort of a "lost grandchild," you can steer the conversation into your areas of interest. Fred has found this to be a way to pull information out of these "storage vaults" that no other means might allow. Just get them talking about the past . . . where people "used to go" and what they "used to do." Of course, never forget to ask these old-timers for any secret tips they have for long life. Who knows, they might direct you to the Fountain of Youth!

Oops, Wrong Road

Don't despair if you missed a turn or read the map improperly. This has happened to everyone! I recall once on vacation when I became almost hopelessly lost on the back roads of North Carolina after heading south out of Williamsburg. But, we weren't in

Look for places like this to hunt for coins . . . an old CCC camp from Depression days located near Pennington, TX. Before the author came, it had probably never been searched before.

a hurry, and no harm was done.

So, "go with the flow" . . . even when you aren't sure where the flow will take you. Just calm down and remember that you really have no choice but to continue driving until you reach the proper route to your destination. Why not take this opportunity to learn about a new section of the country where you find yourself. Benefit from the extra driving. Don't complain about it. Who knows? You may find one or more excellent places to coin hunt that you might never have found on the "right road."

You're really never "lost," you know. In fact, finding your way offers an excellent chance to meet new people when you stop and ask for directions. Even the "crustiest" type will generally warm up to a stranger who admits that he's lost. When you get into conversation with this local resident, you might induce him or her to suggest some nearby coin-hunting spots.

Of course, the excellent road maps now available and the specific markings on all roads and highways throughout the country also insure that you can usually find out where you are quite easily. But, when you happen to find yourself not where you expected to be, take advantage of the situation.

You might spot some rural mailboxes along these back roads. Don't forget to search around them. Country folk used to put coins in the mailbox, along with letters to be picked up by their postal carrier. They probably still do! The coins are for stamps and, sometimes, as a gift for the postman. It was quite common for a coin or two to fall on the ground when the letters were removed from the box. Not all these coins were recovered either! One coin hunter filled a small tin can with Indianhead pennies taken from around these back-country mailboxes.

I asked my brother Don, who was once a rural mail carrier in Angelina County, TX, if he found that coins in rural mailboxes were a thing of the past. "Oh, no," he replied. "Quite often people will leave me coins with a note about what they want to buy with them like stamps and envelopes."

There's your tip! When you find old and deserted farm homes or sites, try to visualize where the mail box may have been and search that area. You may fill your own tin can with Indianheads. Just remember that tampering with the U.S. mail is a federal offense, and never open any mailbox or bother it in any way. In fact, before searching around an active mailbox, you may want to get permission from the owner. Offer him a share of what you find.

Parks for Picnics

Public roadside parks or attractive groves by the side of the road are favorite places for the coin hunter. Search carefully around all tables and benches and out away from them, especially in grassy areas. If there are handrails on which people might have sat or where children could play, be especially thorough in searching under them and as far out as two feet on either side. Scan carefully around drinking fountains, along trails and under trees where people might have lain and rested. Search where cars would have parked for loading and unloading.

Similarly, old camp grounds and fresh water springs are excellent places to find coins as well as to search for lost caches. Many ancient caches are still being found around such areas. At night, when the settlers' wagon trains would stop, families would often bury their wealth to secure it during the night. Because of Indian raids and numerous other tragedies of the trail, some of these travelers never got to recover their possessions. The caches are still there waiting for us treasure hunters.

Search all trails to and from camping grounds. Coins are quite often found around old springs, especially in the water itself. Here is a place where your submersible coil can prove especially valuable. If the encampment sites you are searching are near a river, carefully search the banks both up and downstream from the spot where the river would have been forded. My brother George found a beautiful pair of silver scissors at an old ford on the Neches River in East Texas. These scissors had a cross carved on both sides of the upper handles and the maker's name inscribed in German. Items such as these are worth a high price on today's antique collectors market.

Swimmin' Holes & Beaches

All the various places where people have played in the water probably offer more lost coins, pieces of jewelry and other personal items than any other locations. And, you'll often find as many rings and other pieces of jewelry as coins. Be thorough in your search and by all means let your scanning extend out into the water. Probably *half* of all items lost around swimming areas are lost in the shallow water.

When your detector gives you a signal while you are scanning in the water, mark the location by placing your foot over the "hot spot." Then, using a scoop or shovel with holes in it (to let the water and loose soil drain), bring up a load of mud from under your foot. Slowly lift it to the surface and carefully sift through it, always being alert for broken glass. Because of the vast quantity of things lost in the water and the opportunities there for treasure hunters, an entire chapter in this book is devoted to the search of such areas.

When hunting on a sandy beach, you can speed up your recovery with sieves and wire scoops. They can be dragged along down to a depth of a few inches to recover all solid objects that will not pass through the size mesh you have selected. It's best to make your sieve out of one-half inch wire mesh available at large hardware stores. I have a very efficient three-foot-square sieve I use for sifting sand in swimming and beach areas as well as for sifting where fire has destroyed homes. It is constructed of 2"x4" lumber and half-inch wire mesh. This size mesh was selected so that a dime cannot pass through it diagonally.

Camps & Brush Arbors

Popular fishing spots may yield numerous coins, especially if they included camping grounds as well. You can make discoveries in the areas where campers slept and changed clothes. Always be careful because you'll also find sinkers and fish hooks. Watch out for their sharp points. When you're exploring a fishing camp, try to get into the water where fishermen load and unload their boats. I once found a .22 rifle under two feet of water near a boat launching area. The rifle was in excellent condition even though it had obviously been lost several months before. Apparently it had fallen straight down into the mud which filled up the barrel. This sealed it and prevented water from reaching the riflings to cause rust.

Fishing tackle, fishing boxes and other equipment of all types will be found here. Of course, you'll never want to wade into such areas unless your feet are protected by rugged shoes or boots. Since broken glass abounds here, be especially careful when reaching down into water to retrieve your finds. By the way, whenever you recover a gun, check immediately to see if it is loaded. It probably will be!

Now, for those brush arbors . . . never pass one by! This is an outdoor meeting place, generally where some sort of religious services were observed. Sawdust was often used to cover the earth or other flooring, and long benches were set up for worshipers. For protection from the sun and rain an overhead covering of some sort of brush was used . . . which gave these places their name.

Bill Mahan liked to tell the story of why such spots can be coin hunting bonanzas: "Can't you imagine some old fellow on the hard bench trying not to sleep during a long sermon. But, he does, then finds himself being poked in the ribs as the collection plate is passed. He pulls out some coins and is bound to drop one or two into the sawdust where he groggily tries to find them.

Don't miss the chance to search old park sites like this. Scan around posts, tables and under trees, and always look at the park's edge for paths and trails that lead away from the road.

When he doesn't, we do!"

One of the oldest nickels I ever recovered was found five feet from the front doorstep of an old church. After receiving an excellent signal on my Garrett from our mineral-free East Texas soil, I dug five inches to recover it. When searching around churches, new as well as old, be especially alert in scanning around the doors where adults are most likely to stand talking to one another. You can visualize the scenario yourself as handkerchiefs and cigarettes are pulled from coat and trouser pockets or from handbags. Coins are lost here!

Also search near the rear steps of churches and in and around old trees where children may have played. Quite often, the old country churches had outhouses. The ground around and beneath them should be searched as we have already described. Search in and around areas where people would have parked cars or buggies. Many old churches had picnic areas; make a special effort to locate and search them.

Ghost Towns

Too often, people have a Hollywood or television conception of a ghost town. It's a picturesque old mining community with a great many stores and buildings, and it's now totally desolate and deserted. Nothing like that around my area, you've probably told yourself, and completely ignored the profitable idea of searching ghost towns. But, there are ghost towns in just about every county in the United States!

Surprised? You shouldn't be because a ghost town is just a place where people used to congregate and do business but don't any more. We have lots of ghost towns in the rural areas around Dallas. In some of these there are no structures whatsoever. Crops have been planted or livestock graze where busy communities once thrived. But, regardless, the lost coins and other valuable items are still there waiting to be discovered . . . waiting, that is, until the land is paved over for streets and shopping centers!

So, if you know of one of these nearby *suburban* ghost towns, search it now. Don't procrastinate!

Seek out the locations of old communities and scan over the area thoroughly, whether the ground be bare and deserted or with the structures of an actual town still in place. When searching such a location, some of the better places to look are underneath the boardwalks (or sites of the old boardwalks), out in the streets and thoroughfares and in such money-handling places as stores, banks and saloons. Sometimes it's quite difficult to determine the actual street locations, but there is one method that may be helpful.

The early-day settlements mostly had dirt streets which turned into rivers of mud at the slightest hint of rain. In trying to improve their streets, many of these communities hauled in fill material such as rocks. Tailings provided a good source of rocks at the mining camps! This fill material was often high in iron content, which your metal detector can find quite easily. If you will criss-cross the area in which you believe a community was once located, you can sometimes determine the location of streets by observing the reaction of your detector to the ferrous rocks beneath it. Once you have located the street sites, you can move on to search the walks, stores and houses that stood beside them.

In these early day communities fires were quite common. For example, the famed town of Cripple Creek, CO, was nearly wiped out by a fire. The city rebuilt upon the ruins. If you want to take the time to find the site of burned buildings, it might pay you dividends. Searching the locations of burned buildings and houses sometimes can produce many coins. Often clumps of coins that are melted together will be found. The method used above to locate streets by the ferrous content of fill material can also be used to locate burned-out homesites. Quite often, charred wood and other mineral composition that results from high temperatures during a fire will become conductive. Thus, you can readily locate burned-over sites.

Metal detectors sometimes perform extremely erratically when searching the location of a fire because of the high carbon content of the debris and because there are usually many nails and other pieces of metal present in the soil. Be especially careful of your ground balance when searching such an area. You might be more effective with a smaller searchcoil, as well.

Personal Success Stories

Following are several actual locations where THing pals of mine have found a large quantity of coins. These are listed simply to offer some ideas that may help you select good coin hunting locations of your own:

Karl von Mueller: When the Arizona tourist stop known as Two Gun, east of Flagstaff, burned, over 2,000 coins were found by two coin hunters in the parking area months after the fire. A beginning coin hunter found numerous rings, brooches and bracelets along the waterfront of the Colorado River at Lake Havasu City. Coin hunters with detectors continually find coins under the high bridge across the Rio Grande river west of Taos, NM. When tourists toss coins into the river from high lookouts, prevailing winds blow most of the coins back on the banks of the river. Many of these coins can be found by sight alone, but a detector is needed to make a complete recovery.

Bob Parker: Just below Lake Havasu at Parker, AZ, Bob found nearly $100 in face value of old coins around an abandoned railroad depot and shipping pen area.

Roy Lagal: Roy reports that one of his best areas for locating coins is along the rights of way where wrecking crews have torn down old buildings and houses to make way for new streets and highways. Roy also states that he has also found some surprisingly good caches when he was at construction sites where bulldozers were operating. He adds that with these mechanical "big boys" doing all the hard work for you, it's just necessary sometimes to follow along behind and use your eyes!

Above
Big and valuable money caches such as this are usually buried deeply where they can respond to signals from only the largest searchcoils.
Below
A tree that serves as a fencepost . . . typical marker for a money cache buried long ago that awaits the diligent research efforts of a persistent hobbyist.

These locations, of course, actually represent only a small portion of the good hunting places available to you. The United States is a big and diverse country. Certain activities went on in some parts of our great land and not in others. Industries differed. Recreational pursuits varied from region to region and still do. I'm certain that as you drive around and search different areas and talk with old-timers you will discover new locations. The only limiting factor is the time available to you. So, start today!

Mapping a Search

To help you start may I suggest some terrific maps . . . the topographic maps from the U.S. Geological Survey. They're available to the public for a surprisingly small charge. These topographical maps are printed for just about every area in the United States. They are extremely precise in showing roads, highways, cities, towns and communities. The detail in populated areas is fantastic with all structures, cisterns, wells, windmills and other small landmarks clearly shown and located.

I consider these maps an absolute necessity in treasure and coin hunting. They are ideal for the beginning coin hunter because from these maps he can locate hundreds of possible coin hunting sites within a few miles of his home or along any route he or she plans to travel. A pleasant day or a weekend can be planned from these maps. For further information on maps of the area you desire just call 1-800-USA-MAPS.

Florida beach hunter uses a hand sifter to separate the targets his metal detector has discovered from all the sand that he scooped up in recovering them.

Chapter 10

On the Beaches

S ince the very beginning of time people have flocked to seashores, lakesides and riverbanks in search of pleasure, fun and simply relief from the routine of everyday life. Especially is this true in warmer areas of the United States (and the rest of the world, as well) where the water has always offered an easy form of cooling and one that is still far less expensive than refrigeration! Throughout history people have been drawn to the water . . . to lie in the sun, splash in the surf or swim.

Over the past 25 years, however, an intrepid group has been visiting beaches for entirely different reasons. They seek lost treasure: coins, rings, watches and other jewelry left behind by the sun bathers of today and yesteryear. These treasure seekers with metal detectors are also searching for the gold and silver coins, ingots and artifacts that were originally part of the cargoes of countless wrecked ships that have found their final resting places in shallow offshore coastal waters. The fortunes awaiting such coin and treasure hunters are conservatively estimated to amount to hundreds of millions of dollars.

Silver pieces-of-eight, commonly discovered on Gulf Coast and South Atlantic beaches are a real find for the coin hunter. Sometimes they are found individually; other times they are discovered in bunches or clumps. These pieces of old Spanish and pirate money, usually called *cobs,* get their name from the Spanish *cabo de barra,* or "end of the bar."

The cobs were clipped in succession from the end of a strip of silver. After being trimmed to the proper weight they were placed between two iron or steel dies into which designs for the cobs had been engraved. When forcefully struck, the dies were driven into the metal to produce the finished coin. Silver during this period was minted in denominations of one-half, 1, 2, 4 and

8 *reales.* The 2 and 4-reale pieces became known as "two bits" and "four bits."

Cobs, as well as any siver coins that have lain beneath the sea and sand for many years, are not the bright, shiny specimens found illustrated in coin guides and magazine articles. The chemical action of the salt water and air turns the old Spanish coins into unrecognizable, blackened pieces of metal which must be cleaned to restore them to their "new" condition. Those unfamiliar with the process of corrosion by sea water could walk right past such coins as they lie exposed on the beach. Alert beachcombers can spot the black coins – on the beach and under the sand – with the aid of a modern metal detector.

What Detector?

Not every detector is going to operate for you on an ocean beach, particularly the older models. There's just too much salt water around and too much salt in the sand. In addition, highly mineralized black sand is also present on some beaches. Generally, however, any high quality modern detector will operate satisfactorily whether you use automatic or manual ground balancing. At the approximate discrimination point where iron (ferrous) bottle caps are eliminated from detection, salt water is also eliminated. When scanning on a dry beach, you can scan right out on into the water without experiencing any change in audio threshold.

Even better, there are some detectors manufactured especially for beach and surf hunting. I'm particularly familiar with the Garrett AT4 Beach Hunter which features precise, automatic ground balance and drift-free circuitry. In addition, it's made to withstand a mild dunking and will operate in water depths of a few feet.

Now, for diving you'll have to use special submersible detectors manufactured for that purpose. Garrett makes the Sea Hunter which is certified for leak-free use in water depths to 200 feet. It features pulse induction circuitry and operates very well on the beach. The pulse ignores both salt and black sand.

The pulse induction instruments feature automatic ground balance as do many of the other modern detectors. No ground adjustments are needed. Simply dial in enough discrimination for the types of metal trash you want to eliminate.

Since fresh water does not present the problem of wetted salt, almost any detector will operate near rivers, streams and lakes just about as well as it will in an upland setting.

Spanish Treasure

Along the east coast of Florida and around the Florida Keys are many well documented locations of sunken Spanish galleons. One such area falls near Cocoa Beach, beginning near the town of Sebastian and extending some 35 miles south to a spot just south of Fort Pierce. Here lies the grave of 11 treasure-laden vessels that were trapped by a hurricane while sailing from Havana to Spain in 1715. Their total cargo was valued in excess of tens of millions of dollars, and all but one of the ships sank with everything on board, including most of the seamen.

Immediately following the storm, Spaniards tried to recover the lost valuables. Even with the primitive methods then available, about one-half of them were brought up from the shallow depths of ocean's floor. The remainder lay undisturbed until after World War II. Kip Wagner and a friend found and identified

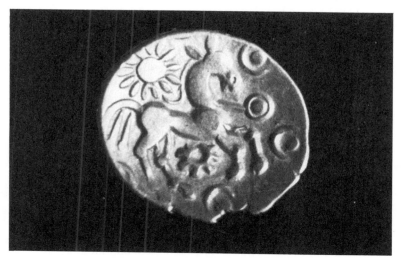

Charles Garrett's personal collection includes this precious gold coin minted approximately 40-20 B.C. Coins such as these are rare indeed, but coins aplenty wait to be found.

several silver coins and formed the Real Eight Corporation to recover sunken treasure. Millions of dollars worth of treasure was recovered by this group, both here and elsewhere, and their pioneering efforts in underwater recovery methods have helped countless others who followed them.

Of course, perhaps the greatest treasure recovery of all time was recorded in the Florida Keys in 1985. Mel Fisher overcame almost insurmountable obstacles, including the death of family members, to find *Nuestra Senora de Atocha,* which sank in 1622. It took him decades of work to find this ship, but the total value of his discovery amounts to hundreds of millions of dollars. All of us at my company are indeed proud that a Garrett Sea Hunter detector was instrumental in discovering the "mother lode" and that our detectors were used extensively throughout his underwater search efforts.

There are many, many other ships still waiting to be found. Some are recorded on the pages of history. Others are not. They await the adventurers daring enough to find them.

Today's Treasures

Well and good, you may say. I've seen the diving movies and watched sharks swimming around. If that's what it takes to find treasure at the ocean, it's not for me!

Well, let me assure you that treasure abounds for any hobbyist who is willing to get his feet and legs wet . . . just occasionally! Even if you insist on remaining dry all over, you can still strike it rich near the water. Any public beach, whether it be ocean, lake or river, is a good place to try your luck. And, in most cases you'll have more luck than you ever imagined . . . provided another coin hunter hasn't beaten you there that day.

That's one of the great advantages of beach hunting. The ocean regularly brings in additional stores of treasures with each new tide. At the same time during vacation and holiday periods more and more people come to the beach to lose coins, jewelry and other precious items. Sun bathers and swimmers will drop coins and shed rings, watches, medallions and all kinds of jewelry in countless numbers. It's easy to understand why!

Take rings, for instance. People go swimming, frolic in the water and play games on the beach in the hot sun. Not only do they perspire, but they make their skin even slipperier with oily creams and lotions. How can anyone expect rings not to slip off into the sand and water? As people swim and splash in the water, throw balls or frisbies and generally engage in horseplay, their rings – and necklaces and bracelets and you-name it – fall to

Pamella Wendel, Florida coin hunter, metal detector hobbyist and beachcomber, has recovered thousands of coins, rings and other items. These below date from the 18th century.

the sand to be quickly mashed down to await the incoming tide . . . or your metal detector!

Of course, when people lose coins, jewelry or other items on the beach, they generally have no idea where they lost them. They've been playing or running around too much! Many of the coins and other objects are carried in a loose pocket of a beach jacket or bathing suit. They could fall out anywhere.

When to Search

The best time to look for coins at the beach is immediately after the weekend or any time after crowds have been there . . . and left. The best time to look for pieces of eight or other items that might have washed ashore from a sunken vessel or ancient shipwreck is immediately after a heavy rainstorm or hurricane. Not only will your coins become uncovered on the beach, but coins that have lain in shallow water will be tossed onto the beach by the roaring waves and high tides.

If you visit beaches or want to add this kind of area to your treasure hunting territory, make it your business to learn where the known productive areas are located. Find out where people go today and where the old wrecks are believed to lie offshore. Where has treasure been found? This is the question that you must answer.

Padre Island, for example, off the southern coast of Texas has been famed for the large quantity of Spanish cobs that have been recovered there. There are even reported finds of original 100-pound Spanish copper containers that were filled with the treasured coins. Much of Padre Island, however, has been placed "off limits" to metal detectors because it is a National Seashore under control of the National Park System. No matter where you search with a metal detector, make certain that you know the local rules and regulations pertaining to use of our instruments. Always remember that ignorance of the law is no excuse!

Most gold items remain fairly well in like-new condition for long periods of time in the ocean. Gold is generally impervious to the chemical action of salt water. Silver in almost all cases turns black after only a few months of exposure. Copper coins sometimes turn green as they slowly corrode. Inexpensive and cheaply plated medallions and similar items will very quickly deteriorate – so quickly, in fact, that after about two or three months they will have been eroded completely away. It is important for you to remember that simply removing the coin or piece of jewelry from salt water does not necessarily stop the corrosive action. It must be cleaned with fresh water and allowed to dry completely.

Where to Search

When you walk out onto a beach, where do you begin? How do you select the most productive areas? This is possibly the question I am asked most frequently by beginning beach hunters (and, more experienced ones as well). The answer, first of all, is that nobody should go pell-mell onto a beach and begin scanning here and there without a plan. This is truly for beginners. There is a right way and a wrong way to search for treasure. As I have stated so often in my books, *"Start right and be successful!"*

You must begin by being in the right place at the right time. What you have already learned about research will suggest sources that will lead you to productive sights. You should also learn about tides and weather so that you will know how you can take advantage of them to put you there at the right time.

The dedicated treasure hunter always first answers the question of "Where?" with research. Beyond that, experience must be the teacher. Inquiring and attentive hobbyists continually pick up ideas from other more veteran beachcombers, but the final decisions must be based on individual perceptions and intuition. Experience alone will educate the beach hunter about places that never produce and other places that are often rewarding. A knowledge of storm, wind and wave action will often rescue someone studying a new beach.

Always begin locally; your home territory is the area you know best. Use every source of leads and information; seek out old timers; visit or write chambers of commerce and tourist bureaus. Don't forget to contact historical societies; leave no source untouched in your investigation of an area. To speed up work always be specific. Ask about information concerning both past and current swimming beaches, resorts and recreational areas. Throughout history, certainly that of this country, swimming has always been a popular activity. Don't overlook the favorite beaches of years gone by, either. Also, ghost towns are not limited to mountainous areas; they can be found on beaches as well. Treasures from the past are always found in and around them.

When checking newspapers, pay particular attention to accident reports that will usually give the location or at least the name of a particular beach. Review old newspapers; be especially alert for the Sunday weekend or recreation columns that proclaim the holiday joys of swimming and sunbathing at local beaches. Advertisements of beachwear occasionally offer clues to areas of activity.

Don't overlook old postcards; antique shops can be a good source. If there is a postcard collector in the area, pay him or her a visit. Old picture postcards can be reliable X-marks-the-spot waybills to treasure.

If you are not a member of your local or regional treasure club, consider joining. If no club exists, get together with other hobbyists and start one! While you can't realistically expect to discover many secret "sweet spots" for finding treasure, you can get to know others who share your interest and enthusiasm. I can assure you that swapping treasure tales and techniques broadens everyone's knowledge, sharpens skills and increases success rates of members. It always helps me!

Search Widely

But, don't let yourself ever become contented with working only local beaches . . . no matter how successful you continue to be in your recoveries! Broaden your scope; it may pay rewards. Never overlook the possibility of finding flotsam and jetsam washing ashore from offshore shipwrecks. Regardless of the age of a wreck, some cargo – especially gold, silver, copper and bronze objects – will probably remain in fair to excellent condition for years, decades or even centuries. Gulf Coast and Caribbean shipwreck locations still yield silver and gold from the mines of Mexico and Peru. Gold and silver from California and other western states can be found along the Pacific coast.

When researching reports of shipwrecks, don't overlook Coast Guard and Life Saving Service records. Newspaper files and local and state histories are good sources of information. Insurance companies and Lloyd's Register may provide precisely the data you need.

Stay alert to current weather conditions. You'll want to search at low tides – the lower the better. After storms come ashore, head for the beach. When oil spills deposit tar and oil on beaches, there's a good possibility bulldozer and other equipment used to remove it can get you much closer to treasure as they remove layers of sand along with the pollution. Watch for beach development work. When pipelines are being laid and when seawalls, breakwaters and piers are being constructed, work these areas of excavation.

I hope these examples of potentially productive areas offer ideas that will encourage you to expand your territory. Coin hunters often travel thousand of miles in their quest for beach treasure. You can do likewise, especially if there is a pot of gold (or *escudos*) at the end of your journey. But, I must stress that considerable local treasure is all around you – wherever you are located. I am positive of this because I know that lost or hidden

Jack Lowry of Garrett helps test new company detectors. He found all of these coins in local parks and on the beaches and surf of the Texas Gulf Coast in carrying out these tests!

coins exist *everywhere*. Find what's in your backyard first; then, hit the treasure trail!

Scanning Tips

Do not race across the sand with your searchcoil waving in front of you. *Slow down!* Work methodically in a pre-planned pattern. Unless you are in a hurry and seek only shallow coins – ones that have just been lost – reduce scan speed to about one foot per second. Let the searchcoil just skim the sands and keep it level throughout the length of a sweep. Overlap each sweep by advancing your searchcoil about one-half its diameter. Always scan in a straight line. This improves your ability to maintain correct and uniform searchcoil height, helps eliminate the "upswing" at the end of each sweep and improves your ability to overlap in a uniform manner, thus minimizing skips. Practice this method; you'll soon come to love it – and, especially its results.

It would be well to mention "hot rocks" here. Gravel on the beach may sometimes include pieces with enough mineral content to be classified as a detectable hot rock. A modern detector occasionally gets a good reading on one of these rocks and sounds off with a "metal" signal. When this happens, set your discriminating mode to zero rejection, switch into that mode and scan back over the gravel. If it is a hot rock, your detector will ignore it, or the sound level will decrease slightly.

Don't ignore either very loud or very faint detector signals. Always determine the source. If a loud signal seems to come from a can or other large object, remove it and scan the spot again. When you hear a very faint signal, scoop out some sand to get your searchcoil closer to the target and scan again. If the signal has disappeared, scan the sand you scooped out – you may have detected a very small target. It might be only a BB, but at least you'll know what caused the signal.

Remember. Your metal detector will never lie to you. When it gives a signal, something is there.

During your search near the water, when you begin detecting trash (pulltabs?) in a line parallel to the waterline, you may have discovered a "trough." If the one you are searching seems to contain primarily trash, search for a nearby parallel trough.

Remember that more than one trough may have been created, and that those farther out can contain heavier treasure items. Walk out from your "trash trough" and seek out one that produces keepers.

When pinpointing, always try to be precise. Good pinpointing saves time and lessens the possibility of damaging your finds when you dig.

When Joe Maenner of Fort Worth was in the Air Force in Washington, he had above average coin-hunting luck at such beaches as Coeur D'Alene and Rocky Point. And, he discovered an old swimming beach near Post Falls, ID. The total of his finds there consisted of almost 2900 coins, ten wedding rings, 12 birthstone rings, 37 religious medals and 16 assorted jewelry items. He said that the coins were so numerous that many of them were simply lying in view when the water was low. He searched during winter months through snow and over ground that was sometimes frozen.

Protect Your Instrument

No matter where you are searching, always think of the scientific instrument that you are using. True, it's built to withstand rugged outdoor treatment, but sand on most beaches is quite fine and is blown around through the air quite vigorously. Most beach hunters are able to pour out surprisingly large quantities of sand from their instruments after each journey to the oceanside. If you're using a conventional detector, you might want to carry along a plastic bag to slip over the detector housing. Cut out holes for the control knobs, earphone jack and speaker, if necessary.

Of course, if you're using a detector like the Beach Hunter that is specially designed for searching the beaches you won't have this problem with sand . . . or water, either.

Speaking of water. *Never* submerge a conventional detector in any kind of water. And, be careful about laying it down at the water's edge where a wave might splash over it. Now, I'm aware of stories told about drying out an instrument properly and having it operate again after it's gotten a bath of fresh water. Factory technicians all agree, however, that they know of no instance of a conventional detector ever being submerged in salt water and operating properly again . . . especially if it was turned on when it went under the sea! Of course, you never want to place a detector or searchcoil in an oven for drying. Normal temperature is sufficient.

Don't forget the stem of your detector. Make certain that it is clean and free of sand after a beach expedition. It's possible that you may have to wash it with soap and water. Always take care to drain the stem properly so that water is not retained in it. This can sometimes flow back into your detector housing if the detector is tilted upwards.

The noises of the ocean's roar, racing waters or crowds of people make headphones almost mandatory in beach hunting. Of course, most veteran coin hunters will recommend that you *always* wear headphones to make certain that you miss no weak or fringe signals. Headphones enhance audio perception by bringing the sound directly into a coin hunter's ears while masking outside noise interference. More information concerning audio and headphones is contained in Chapter 19.

Finally, remember that a modern metal detector is a wonderful scientific instrument for locating lost coins on the beach . . . or anywhere else. It searches beneath the sand, where you cannot see. It is always vigilant about the presence of metal. But, no detector can "do it all." You must develop powers of observation that keep you attentive to what a detector cannot see. Especially on the beach should you watch for the unusual! Sometimes you'll visually locate money, marketable sea shells or other valuables. The real benefit of developing keen powers of observation, however, is to enable you to enjoy the glories of the beach to their fullest and never to overlook the signposts pointing to detectable treasure.

As you scan along the waterline and observe the sands under the water, you may eye a coin shining in the water. Check the spot with your detector. Perhaps you found only a freshly dropped coin, or it could be the top layer of much greater treasure. And, how about that rock outcropping, the gravel or shells peeking through the sand, that accumulation of debris . . . any of these might mark the location of a glory hole. Remain alert and be rewarded!

As you may have gathered by now, I'm enthusiastic about

hunting with a metal detector on the beaches and in the water. My recent book, *Treasure Recovery from Sand and Sea,* is totally dedicated to this pastime. If you're interested in learning more about the use of metal detectors in and near the water, I suggest you read it. Regardless, however, I urge you to believe me when I tell you that there's treasure to be found near the water! And, vast amounts are waiting . . . enough for all. I sincerely hope that you'll join the rest of us beachcombers in searching for this lost and hidden wealth.

Facing

Above
Robert Marx has searched shipwrecks under waters all over the world with Garrett metal detectors to find vast amounts of valuable treasure.

Below
Garrett metal detectors are suitable for seeking treasure anywhere on the face of the earth or anywhere under its waters (to depths of 200 feet).

Over
On the sands of Padre Island, TX, this pretty girl finds coins successfully with the same underwater detector that she had earlier used in the surf.

114

Chapter 11
Digging Coins

So, you've done your research and found your "hot spot." You've used the right kind of detector and have a strong signal. You're positive that you've located a good coin or something even more valuable. It's pinpointed and shows *gold* on your meter.

What next?

Well, *dig,* of course. And, what kind of advice have you heard about digging coins? How about these good suggestions:

"Don't use a screwdriver . . . it'll scratch!"

"Never use a knive . . . you'll ruin the sod!"

"Always use a probe . . . less damage to the sod!"

"Don't scratch your coin with a probe!"

Sounds confusing, doesn't it? Well, let me confuse you just a little more by telling you that *all* of the above advice can be good

Facing
These handsome "pieces of eight" were recovered from a Spanish treasure ship off the coast of Florida by a diver using a Sea Hunter detector.

Over
Above
Wallace Chandler shows Charles Garrett a sampling of the many treasures he has recovered with a metal detector from beaches and bodies of water.
Below
Glorious discoveries beckon hobbyists with metal detectors. You might not find something with every sweep of a searchcoil, but treasures galore await.

. . . it just depends on what you're digging for and in what kind of turf you're digging! The problem coin hunters face when it comes time to dig is that each type of soil requires, generally, a different digging and retrieval technique. Retrieving coins from the sandy beach, of course, is perhaps the easiest. Digging coins out of hard-packed clay under dense St. Augustine grass may be the most difficult. Retrieval in good, loose dirt under a growth of Bermuda grass lies somewhere between the two extremes.

My coin-hunting expeditions have taken me from frozen turf in the Far North to sandy Caribbean beaches, and I've stopped at lots of places in between. So, I understand a great many of the different techniques. But, they must be learned by any coin hunter who wants to hunt with maximum efficiency. I wish I could tell you that somewhere in these journeys I had discovered a magic solution for digging. But, there is none. It just represents work . . . sometimes, harder than at other times . . . but, always work. The only consolation is that there is often a fine and immediate reward for the work!

When I first wrote this chapter, I decided to ask a number of the coin hunters . . . men and women whose ideas and opinions I respect . . . to contribute their thoughts on digging. I suppose I was secretly hoping that one of them had discovered the *magic*. Alas, none had. But, they produced such an excellent general discussion of recovering coins as well as presenting a number of interesting techniques for digging in specific types of soils that I want to offer their ideas again (with just a little bit of updating).

When I included these ideas in the first book, I preceded them with an admonition, and I repeat what I wrote 15 years ago:

"You will note in reading through this chapter that several of the coin hunters use different methods in either probing or retrieving. Keep in mind these people have worked out their *own* recovery techniques for speed, ease of recovery, less damage to coins and sod. One method which may work over one given type of sod may not be the best for another type. A method that one person may *love* could be totally unsatisfactory for somebody else. Study them all; practice them all; and select the method you prefer in the area you work."

To this I can add in 1989 only the word, "Amen!"

Wendel's Sand

Bill and Pamela Wendel live very close to miles and miles of lovely Florida beaches where many tourists come to swim, sun bathe, frolic and hunt coins. Of course, they all lose coins, jewelry and other valuable personal items . . . everyone loses things – even the metal detector hobbyists. The Wendels have worked out a technique for the recovery of these lost objects. They use two tools, a wire mesh scoop-sifter and a small plastic trowel something like a sugar scoop.

When they have pinpointed the metallic object with their detector they can make one pass through the sand with the sifter if the sand is loose and fine. Zingo! The object is in the sifter, just waiting for the loose sand to be shaken out. Unfortunately, this method doesn't work too well in wet, saturated sands near the water. Here's where the trowel is brought into play.

After pinpointing, they insert the trowel several inches into

Charlie Weaver and Roy Lagal break through snow and ice to search this park in the Nez Perce Indian reservation. Specially designed picks are used to penetrate the frozen ground.

121

the ground and with one quick twist "plug" the beach sand, remove the plug and retrieve the coin in it. Rarely do either of the Wendels attempt any digging with bare hands in either dry or wet sand. They admit that it's quite a temptation, especially in fine, loose sand that looks so warm and inviting. But, *there's just too much broken glass* and other sharp objects that will cut into fingers and hands. How about gloves? Pamela says that they're too hot. So, it's the sifter and trowel for the Wendels in the sands of Florida's beaches.

Smith's Half Circle

Bill Smith and his wife number their coin finds in the tens of thousands with hundreds upon hundreds of rings and other valuables. When he locates a coin in the low-mineral soil of his Oklahoma hunting grounds, he cuts a half-circle around it and makes it three inches deep. Then, he folds the turf back. If the coin isn't in this first plug, he removes a second and deeper plug, making certain that all loose dirt falls back into the hole. After he retrieves the coin, he folds the turf back in place and steps on it.

He reports that this method is especially good with Bermuda grass which tends to die when you cut a full circle in the grass. Seems to kill the roots, Bill observes. Of course, he never puts trash back in holes for someone else to dig up. That's why Bill Smith always wears an apron with two pockets . . . one for keepers and one for trash.

The Nutmeg State

Connecticut coin hunter Mike Kramptiz recommends that, if you must cut a plug, that you cut it square so that it will fit precisely back into the hole. He suggests further that the plug be cut deeply with lots of soil attached to it so that powerful lawnmowers can't pull your plug from the ground before the grass has become re-established. He believes that cone-shaped (pointed at the bottom) plugs are more likely to be uprooted by mowers. Also, he adds that you might want to try to pinpoint your coin in the plug itself after you dig it up. Then, removal can be more exact, and you won't have to break apart the plug to find your target. He believes that the more dirt that is left on the plug, the more likely the grass is to live.

Using a Screwdriver

Of course, a screwdriver is one of the most popular tools used today for coin retrieval. A well known hunter on the East Coast submitted this method for digging and recovering coins faster, better and with less damage to sod than with any other tool he's ever used. After pinpointing, he pushes the screwdriver into the ground about two to three inches behind the coin. He sticks it in at a 45-degree angle about five inches deep. Of course, he uses a screwdriver with a *dull* point to keep from scratching a coin if he should accidentally punch the point into his find. Now, with his screwdriver inserted five inches deep he pushes forward and to the left, making a slit in the ground three to five inches long. Then he makes the same slit to the right, with the two slits leaving a "vee-shaped" piece of sod. He pushes the vee-shaped chunk of sod forward with his hand, swinging it up out of the ground. He reports that after you have retrieved your coin, the sod will fall back into the hole in the exact place it came out, and the grass roots will not die. Also, he does not cut roots of the grass by making his "V," but merely pulls most of the roots through the ground. This successful hunter is convinced that most park caretakers would much rather see coin hunters use a screwdriver than a knife!

Another Method

Here's a slightly different retrieval method for use in parks and other areas where the hobbyist must be careful not to damage the sod. After pinpointing, carefully insert your dull-pointed probe into the ground until you touch the coin. This will inform you of its exact depth. Then insert a heavy duty screwdriver in the hole made by your probe, but stop before it touches the coin. (Remember, you already know how deeply buried it is!) Rotate the screwdriver gently until you have a cone-shaped hole about three inches in width across the top. It is then usually an easy matter to remove the coin with just a little digging with your fingers or the point of the screwdriver. This method requires some practice and skill, especially when probing, because the coin must not be scratched. To fill the hole, insert the screwdriver into the ground two or three times around the opening. With just a small pressure toward the hole the surrounding soil and grass fill it in, leaving absolutely no scar.

Charlie Weaver's Probe

Charlie Weaver of Lewiston, ID, uses a stainless steel probe with a diameter a little larger than the wire of a coathanger. The point is carefully rounded and smoothed so that it will not scratch a coin's surface. Charlie has been coin hunting for many years in Idaho and has amassed a beautiful collection of coins, rings and other valuables that must be kept in a bank vault! I've watched Charlie hunt for coins, and I agree that his method is a good one. It is exact, precise and quick. He is very adept at pinpointing with his detector and then locating the coin with his probe.

I watched Charlie get a signal and pinpoint a target. He inserted the probe into the ground and touched the coin on the first insertion. He cut a cone-shaped plug, removed it from the ground and pulled out a 1906-O quarter from the bottom of his plug. Believe it or not, this quarter was buried four inches deep, standing vertically! Remember, I said the first time he inserted the probe, he *touched* the coin. With the quarter standing on edge, I would say that was a tremendous feat of detector pinpointing.

Charlie scoffs at the many people who warn him about using a probe . . . who caution about scratching coins and ruining their value. He admits that he scratched a coin or two when he first began probing but says that he can now tell instantly when he touches the coin and rarely mars one. Futhermore, he finds that by probing first he can determine the exact depth and position of the coin which lets him recover his finds quickly and precisely. He admits that tree roots and pieces of glass sometimes cause problems but experience has taught him how to deal with them.

Making a Probe

Another Idaho treasure hunter, "Pinky" Nobel offers instructions on how to construct a coin probe. Cut a piece of 3/32-inch piano wire approximately 12 inches long. Cut a lengh of broom stick about four and one-half inches long. Then, drill a 3/32-inch hole down the center of this handle four inches deep. Force the piano wire into the hole all the way to the bottom. Round off the end of the wire until it is smooth, and check it regularly to make certain it remains smooth. Probe carefully, he warns.

Bill Fangio's Lawns

Bill Fangio, who designed a great deal of electronic metal detector equipment in his day, was always aware of the problems of finding coins in a well-manicured lawn . . . one where no one is normally permitted to dig a hole. For those areas he suggested a method that is acceptable to most any lawn caretaker. It's a little slower than plugging, but it gets the job done!

After pinpointing, carefully probe with a rounded point until you locate your coin. Then, with the probe still in the ground, approximately an inch or two out from the probe, select a screwdriver with about an 8-inch shaft. Insert it deep enough to place the tip slightly below the tip of the probe. Remove the probe and carefully work your coin to the surface with the tip of the screwdriver.

Now, I'll admit that this method can be difficult to use at first,

Just a tiny slit in the ground was all this coin hunter needed to recover a find. Numerous successful methods for digging and recovery are described in detail in this chapter.

125

but with practice it becomes easier. If you hunt in areas where you are not permitted to plug the grass, you should learn how to use this method. You might try experimenting by bending the tip of a screwdriver slightly to form a small scoop. In some types of soil this screwdriver/scoop helps retrieve the coin. It's a lot harder to use Bill's method than just slicing into the grass and removing a plug, but it may enable you to recover some old and valuable coins that would otherwise remain beneath a beautiful, manicured lawn.

Other Methods

There you have seven different methods for probing for and/or retrieving buried coins. There are other methods you can use depending upon the soil condition. In extremely hard and sun-baked soil and in frozen ground it is necessary to use some type of wide-blade pick to actually hack your way into the ground. In softer dirt the digging is easier, and one of the methods described above or your own variation of it might prove to be more practical and less damaging to the ground.

Regardless of the type of ground where you plan to hunt, you should study all these methods and work out the one or ones best suited to your needs. Remember, soil conditions can be expected to change with the weather as well as with geography. Be prepared, no matter where you hunt.

Good luck with your digging, and always remember to *fill those holes!*

Your Tools

Of course, your most important tool will be a high quality metal detector. This subject is discussed quite fully in Chapters 18 through 20, including a discussion of the price you should expect to pay for the correct instrument.

Your second most important accessory will be the tools with which you choose to dig. Among the useful tools that you will need for locating and recovering coins are probe, knife, screwdriver, weed sickle, apron with at least two pockets, small flashlight, old trash box and–don't laugh–a lawnmower. You will soon learn why you will require different types of digging tools for different types of ground conditions. A weed sickle or cutter is a handy item to have because quite frequently you will encounter bushes and clumps of grass you must remove in order to scan an area properly. If you search at night, you may need a flashlight. The trash box is good for dumping your trash into when there are no trash containers available.

Now, I'm not suggesting by any means that each coin hunter carry around a big power lawn mower. (Maybe you could *ride* to your hunting location on it!) But, seriously, I would venture to guess that the day will come when you would gladly mow the lawn of an abandoned church or the lawn around an old house in order to search for lost coins, since it is at these locations that you will find the older and more valuable ones.

You will definitely need a small bag suspended from your belt or a coin-hunting apron with at least two pockets, made either of waterproof plastic or with plastic pocket liners. Quite often you will be digging in areas that are wet. When you retrieve coins from the ground, especially muddy ground, some of the soil will stay with the coin until you have had an opportunity to clean it. This accumulation of damp soil can cause the contents of non-waterproofed pockets to leak through onto your clothing.

Always carefully determine into which pocket you will be placing valuable finds and into which one you will be placing the trash (bottle caps, nails, pop tops, foil and such). Recover and properly dispose of all junk you find because it is likely you will return to the same spot to search again, or *another coin hunter* will try his luck there. Even if you don't return, the complete absence of metal in the ground will alert future coin hunters that this area has already been searched.

In addition, caretakers will love you because you are helping keep their park clean. Often, when these persons learn what you are doing and realize you are actually helping them clean their park, they will give you valuable information you can use to find coins more successfully. They may be able to tell you where people have congregated and, consequently, where coins are most likely to be found. They can tell you the former location of picnic tables, playground equipment and other centers of activity that might help you locate "hot spots."

Write It Down

Always carry a pen or pencil and paper with you to make notes of your finds and ideas that come to mind as you hunt coins. In coin hunting, like anything else, you learn by doing. As you hunt, you will discover your mistakes, and you will develop your own particular style with new and better ways to find and recover coins.

From the beginning of your coin hunting career get into the habit of "logging in" your finds. You should keep track of not only the good stuff you find but also the junk. As you become more experienced with your detector, you will be able to observe the growth of your proficiency. When this begins to happen, you'll notice the ratio of "good" to "bad" finds increasing on the "good" side. The better you understand your detector's signal, the more junk you will be able to leave in the ground. Thus, a daily record is valuable to show your progress and allow you to keep score as you watch accumulations of coins and other valuables grow day by day.

Chapter 12

Underwater Recovery & Dredges

I n this chapter I will present briefly both detector and suction dredge underwater recovery techniques. Many people are now utilizing their detectors and dredges to clean out swimming and recreational underwater sites. If you are fortunate enough to find one or more of these locations that has gone unworked, your rewards should be great. It is estimated that more than one-half of all coins, rings, jewelry and other valuable items that are lost at recreation and swimming sites are lost in the water; the other half, of course, are lost on the beach or shore.

If you're using your detector to search on the beach, don't be afraid to take it out into the water—just be sure to protect it from submersion or even heavy splashing unless it's a surf-hunting model designed to be dunked. Your searchcoils are probably submersible (all those made by Garrett are), but always check to make certain. If your searchcoil is submersible, you can use it in the water just so long as the searchcoil connector on the detector housing does not become wet. Of course, when you're in water that's over a foot or two deep, recovery becomes a problem.

About Recovery

Only one thing really separates the water hunter from the land hunter . . . the surf hunter from the beach hunter. And, that's *recovering* a find. Because a hobbyist simply can't see under the water (most of the time, at least), more attention must be given to digging techniques, target analysis and other aspects of recovery. Among these, even, are the clothes a surf hunter wears and the pouches in which finds are stored! There's

129

a big difference between recovering coins on land and in the water.

Yet, the principles of recovery are the same no matter where you discover coins. You have to work out some means of removing your find from where it lies hidden. When your detector signals a coin under sand lying four feet beneath ocean waves, recovery is considerably different – and more difficult – than in a park or playground.

Let's now consider just what tools you'll need for these more difficult recoveries in deeper water and the other types of equipment required by surf hunting that you might find different from that used in traditional treasure hunting with a metal detector.

Equipment that you will need will, of course, depend upon whether you work in shallow or deep-water surf. We can define shallow surf as water depth that permits you to dig with your hands, a hand scoop or a tool – in other words, at arm's length. Deep water surfing is hunting in depths to about five feet, or the maximum depth you can safely wade in the water without swimming or floating.

Your choice of retrieving tools will depend upon soil conditions and personal preferences. In sandy areas, a scoop is the fastest. If the soil is muddy or made of hardened clay, you will need some kind of digger. In deep water, a long-handled scoop is required to retrieve your finds, sometimes in combination with a digger.

When the water grows colder, hip or chest-high waders and suitable underclothing will keep you warm and dry. When wearing waders, be alert or else you may bend over too far. Suddenly, you'll find yourself wearing "convertible" gear. Your waders have been "converted" into a wet suit! Wearing a waist or chest belt over waders can reduce the amount of water that comes in.

Must Close Tightly

It's a good idea to make certain that whenever you're hunting in or near the water that you use treasure pouches that can be closed securely to keep coins and other valuable objects (also trash) from "floating off" if your pouch happens to become submerged. The open-pocket apron will not be satisfactory in the water!

No matter what type of treasure pouch or pouches you use, they must close tightly with a secure flap covering. Some surfers use a sturdy open-weave bag or a pouch with zipper or drawstring. Whatever equipment your ingenuity comes up with, keep it in good shape. And, check its condition regularly. Don't lose valuables through holes! Just as your apron in the park, your water-hunting pouch should have several pockets that let you separate treasure and trash. But, whatever you do, never discard trash without carefully examining every piece. While standing in knee-deep surf with waves splashing around you, you may have inadvertently placed a good find in the trash pocket. Also, that item that looked so corroded and unrecognizable may turn out to be a valuable object. When in doubt about any find, take it home for closer examination, even an electrolytic bath for cleaning.

Some surfers use a flotation screen; others do not. If you use a converted land metal detector, you'll need a flotation device unless you mount the detector control housing on your body, or on the end of a very long searchcoil stem. The flotation device, of which there are several designs, is constructed with a one-half inch sturdy chicken wire screen. The screen opening should not allow a U.S. dime to pass through diagonally. If you are searching for smaller objects, the screen openings should be even smaller. If your flotation device is large or contains your detector's control housing, the screen portion should hinge to permit rapid dumping of accumulated trash. The float can have recesses for the detector, a water bottle, your lunch and, perhaps, an extra tool or other necessity. Select a tube from the various automobile, motorcycle or bicycle sizes available. Since you are really not supporting much weight, the tube does not have to be highway bus or truck size. You should position the screen so that its bottom surface is about one or two inches below the water line. This facilitates quick washing of debris, mud and sand. In fact, when you dump several scoops into a well-designed flotation device, wave action should quickly clean the material.

Some hunters have said they prefer to place several scoops of dug material into their screen before they examine its contents and retrieve their finds. This can be efficient when you're using a zippered bag which takes extra time to open and close each time you store a find. If the bottom is heavy silt and mud, it also might be quicker to dissolve and inspect a large of amount of soil rather than stir through your smaller retrieving scoop each time you make a dig.

Using a Float

Of course, always remember that an innertube can be punctured accidentally. This is a problem only if your detector housing is mounted on the float. Even then, I think you would hear the air escaping and you could rescue the detector before it got a bath. Placing your detector on a float is not recommended, however, for several other reasons. It has no protection from rain, the occasional wave or water splashed by swimmers.

When I'm looking for coins on loose sandy bottom sites, I do not use a floating screen. As I begin bringing up the scoop filled with sand and other bottom objects, I immediately begin shaking the scoop. By the time I have it up to the water's surface, most, if not all, of the sand has already fallen through the holes.

You *must* tether a float to yourself or you'll lose it. According to Murphy's (infallible) Law, the first time you turn your back on an untethered float, it will set sail for faraway places and head straight out to sea. You can probably tell that I'm not much of a fan of floats. I consider having to manipulate a detector and a long-handled scoop problem enough. Plus, it is not practical to use a float in surf areas when the waves are high. It will be constantly banging into you. And, it will never be where you want it when you need it.

Also, in using a large open-basket screen, you invite thievery. Some individuals are naturally tempted when they see valuables lying in an open screen. Carl Rattigan and I were once working a Guadeloupe surf when several boys swam up to watch. Carl brought up a scoop that contained what he described as "the most beautiful and valuable gold medallion of the week!" A boy reached into the scoop, grabbed the medallion and darted off with it through the waves.

There are those surf hunters who swear by floats that are constructed entirely of non-metallic materials. With such floats the hunter can scan an entire float with a detector to make certain that no mud balls and other encrustrations contain coins or other treasures. While that idea certainly has some merit, I do not consider it the most efficient method. I recommend that you investigate by hand and then scan every strange item you discover. And, as I have said, take every "unknown" object home for closer scrutiny.

I've seen surf hunters use handmade "sifting baskets," which they sling on their hip. With an opening large enough to dump a scoop's entire contents into, this seems to work quite well.

Retrieving Tools

Your scoop and all retrieving tools must be ruggedly constructed. You will be putting a lot of force on your scoop each time you make a dig. A plastic scoop . . . even one that works satisfactorily on the beach . . . may not stand the strain beneath the water. As for your long-handled scoop, its upper end should have a screw, lanyard, paint stripe or other marker to let you know at a glance on which side the scoop opening is located. You don't want to have to waste time pulling it out of the water just to locate the open end so you'll know how to dig with it properly. A "looped" handle (one whose handle is formed by rods extending from both the top and bottom of the scoop itself to form a closed loop at the top) is the configuration I prefer. Further, the scoop's rear handle section should be curved backward so that you don't have to lean too far forward to tilt the scoop into the required vertical position for proper digging. When you push the handle forward to position the scoop vertically, your hand should be about midway or lower down the rear handle. Then, you begin your backward pull while sliding your hand upward. You'll also rotate the handle slightly to free the scoop from the muck. As you bring the handle backwards, you'll slide your hand over the top to the front rod of the handle and grasp it as close to the scoop as possible. You then pull the scoop free of the bottom. This low position of your hand on the forward rod of the handle keeps the open end of the scoop upright so that nothing falls out. Shake the scoop as you bring it up to let sand and small debris work through its holes.

When working in shallow water (arm's length-depth or less)

use a scoop or digger, depending on bottom material and density. When the material is light, you can fan it away by hand or speed up the action with a ping pong paddle. Be observant when you are fanning since lighter junk items such as pulltabs or even small coins can float away with the sand. Of course, the pulltabs are certainly no loss, but you may just keep detecting them over and over again. When you've set your discrimination control to pulltab rejection, however, you'll know that a pulltab can't be that "coin" you just detected. Keep fanning and watch for a coin or some other metallic object to appear.

In deep water, use one of the following scoop-retrieving methods. First, you must pinpoint the detected object. Then, bring the scoop forward and lightly touch the back edge of the searchcoil. Move the searchcoil out of the way and tilt the scoop forward and press on the butt end of the scoop with your foot. Now, I don't particularly like this method because the detector's loud *squeeeeel* when the metal scoop comes near its searchcoil gets on my nerves. Plus, battery power is wasted. So, I use one of the other methods.

After detector pinpointing, some hunters place their foot lightly on top of the searchcoil, then move the coil away. They can place the scoop adjacent to their shoe to achieve correct scoop positioning.

Still another method is to place your left foot beside the searchcoil and move the searchcoil away to the right. Then, lower the scoop until it touches the inside heel of your left shoe in the correct position for retrieval.

Facing

Digging in wet sand is often harder than it looks, and this hobbyist is using a small pick to make certain she avoids glass and other sharp objects.

Over

What a wonderful find . . . and what a precise job of pinpointing and digging permitted her to recover it without making a mess of this handsome lawn.

Practice . . . Practice . . .

Regardless of the method you use, practice until you have achieved perfection, even digging several scoop depths, if necessary. Don't worry if you have to try several times at first to retrieve your coin. It comes easier with practice. If you occasionally keep "losing" an item, the object may have been small enough to slip through your scoop holes. I had this problem once when I was digging everything (All Metal mode) at a beach site in Antigua. The objects that I was "losing" turned out to be ladies' hairpins. Placing a magnet near the bottom of the scoop to attract these iron objects will overcome this problem.

If you get a signal, but fail to scoop up a target on the first try, pinpoint it again with your detector. If the target moved, it could be a small object that sifted through the scoop. If you cannot locate it with your detector, it may be a deep coin or ring that turned edgewise when the scoop contacted it. Try digging deeper to see if you can locate those mysteriously "lost" objects.

Here's a phenomenon to observe while surf hunting: Remember the science classes of your school days when you learned about diffraction or the "bending" of light? This occurs when light passes through a water/air boundary. An underwater object such as your searchcoil will thus appear to be in a different place from where it actually sits. Until you get used to it, this sighting error may cause you to misjudge the location of your searchcoil in relation to your scoop.

Facing

Recovering coins from all types of soil is one of the many aspects of the hobby that must be studied and practiced before success can be achieved.

Over

These treasures came from "Nuestra Senora de la Regla," where they were found by Charles Garrett's friend Roy Volker using a Sea Hunter detector.

Considerably more space has been devoted to beach and surf hunting in this new book on coin hunting than I used in my original edition 15 years ago. That's true for several reasons. First is simply the personal success I've had at beach and surf hunting . . . the coins and other valuable items that I have found over the past decade and one-half. If I can be successful, so can you. The second reason is because of the fine new detectors we have developed that can hunt as well on the beach as anywhere else; wetted salt and black sand don't bother them. In addition are the new models such as our AT4 Beach Hunter that are made specifically for the beach.

Finally, new and better equipment of all kinds is permitting our hobby to expand into the new frontiers of water hunting. This equipment includes not only modern detectors with ground balancing and environmental protection adequate for satisfactory operation in salt water but new and better scoops and other recovery apparatus. More and more traditional coin hunters are discovering a new and exciting world *beyond the water's edge*.

Yes, all of this is good! Coins can be found on the beach and in the surf to an extent that you've never imagined. If you're truly interested in this exciting phase of our hobby, please take the time to read my just-published *Treasure Recovery from Sand and Sea*. It will give you a totally new insight into the use of a metal detector in and near the water.

Dredges

Because there are so many coins and other attractive targets in the water, the use of dredges for recovering them has become more popular. While dredges are built primarily for prospectors and placer mining operations, they can be used effectively in the water of a swimming beach. If you are successful in locating and dredging some of the old swimming areas, of which there are thousands throughout the United States, you could quite easily pay for your all of your dredging equipment from just one of these clean-out operations.

A simple suction dredge consists of a gasoline-powered engine (like the one on your lawnmower), a water pump usually connected directly to the motor shaft and a suction hose with a nozzle. With the engine driving the pump, suction is created at the nozzle which causes not only water but also mud, rocks, coins – anything else small enough to go through the nozzle – to be pulled through the hose and deposited on a "riffle board" in a sluicebox on the floating dredge itself. The riffle board is ridged to collect the heavier objects, such as gold nuggets and large coins which are sucked up by the pump. Heavier objects fall into the troughs between the ridges while the water's force tumbles

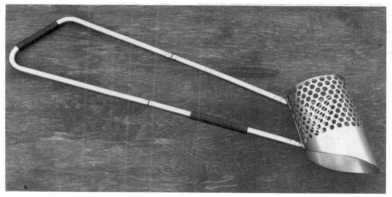

Charles Garrett's favorite surf recovery scoop, designed by his friend Alden Fogliadini, is both sturdy and versatile. As shown below, three handles are used for varying water depths.

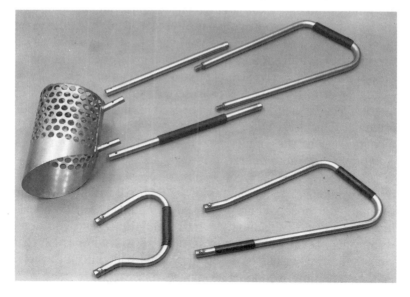

the small rocks, mud balls and other lighter material over the board and back into the water.

When used on swimming beaches, suction dredges will suck up lost coins, rings, watches and similar valuables to be deposited on the riffle board or in a wire mesh basket. My dredge is equipped with such a basket which permits water, sand and small objects to pass through the mesh back into the water. One person can operate a small dredge in shallow water, but two people are usually required for the most efficient operation. One person uses the nozzle and the other keeps an eye on the water and other material as it all flows over the board through the sluicebox or into the mesh basket. You'll want to set aside your good finds so that sand and water can pass through the sluicebox more easily. Broken glass and fish hooks, among other trash, will also be brought up in the hose. Look out for them! When in rivers and lakes you can also expect an occasional snake to be sucked up. 'Nuf said!

Different Sizes

Dredges are classified according to the diameter of the inside of the suction nozzle and hose. The size of the nozzle opening is always smaller than the hose diameter to create good suction and limit the size of items that are pulled up through it. Consider the size carefully when you are buying a dredge. Determine what is the largest size object you want to retrieve and buy a dredge with a rating at least one-half inch greater than the diameter of that object. The size of your dredge can present a "two-edged sword" to you. You can recover greater quantities of material more rapidly with a larger dredge, but the larger sizes are more difficult to operate. It's quite possible for one person to manage one of the smaller-sized units, but the bigger ones *demand* two or more operators.

Of course, your major concern is to recover all valuable finds while maintaining an adequate flow of material from the bottom through your hose and into the dredge. You can't let the nozzle become clogged by jamming it into the bottom, and you don't want your basket or sluicebox so filled with sand or trash that coins and other valuable objects flow right back into the water. At the same time, you must always be very careful to keep your float balanced. It must sit level in the water for the dredge to operate properly. If you mount the engine too far to one side, the float will tip in that direction. Also, always be careful when using a pneumatic tube for a float. The right kind of puncture leaves you with a "sinking" dredge instead of a "floating" one!

Dredges should be operated at about one-half to one-third of maximum engine and pump speed. This is adequate to bring coins up easily. If there is too much pressure, they can shoot right through your sluicebox over the riffles and back into the water. Since these coins could be discolored, you might never notice them. Now, wire mesh screening can protect you to an extent, but it slows down operations since you must constantly be cleaning debris out of the screen or basket. It's a good idea to

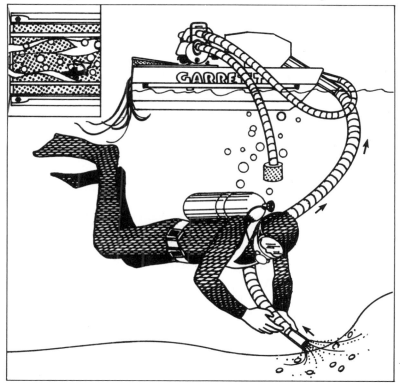

A dredge literally "lifts" the bottom of a swimming area through its nozzle and carries it to the surface for inspection and recovery of coins, jewelry and other valuable objects.

position a screen about half-way down your sluicebox to prevent coins from being tumbled back into the water.

Some final suggestions: An extension pole can be used to extend the nozzle for dredging in deeper water. Never start your dredge without water in the pump; it could burn out before you know it! Always test your dredge to make certain it's operating satisfactorily before taking it into deep water. It's mighty frustrating to be "cranking" a balky engine while standing in waist-deep water!

Some Tips

Here are some places where coins have been successfully dredged. This list is not intended to recommend that you go to one of these places. Far from it; in fact, some of these may already be "dredged out" – if that's ever possible. Rather, this list is to suggest the type of locations you can develop for yourself.

Royal Gorge, CO – In the Colorado River underneath this famed bridge and tourist stop thousands of coins of all denominations have been recovered as well as occasional rings, bracelets and watches. Of course, the coins have usually been tossed off the high bridge for "good luck." Unfortunately for the tosser, his luck is sometimes immediately "bad" since rings, bracelets and watches are accidentally flung along with coins.

Astoria, OR – There's a famous Wishing Bridge here similar to the Royal Gorge bridge noted above. Metal detectors have been used along the banks and in the stream bed with some success even though coins are sometimes damaged from rocks.

Atlantic Resort Beaches – Numerous popular beaches along the Atlantic Coast have been worked with dredges with varying degrees of success. Some hobbyists first "scout" a beach's surf area with a metal detector. If goodly numbers of coins are found, a dredge is brought in for a more complete and far more rapid underwater recovery.

Brown County, IN – Gold dredges in streams in southern Indiana occasionally find a small amount of coins, a retrieval that is mysterious since nobody can figure out how the coins got here.

Canadian River, NM – For a quarter of a mile downstream from the Highway 85 bridge, hundreds of coins have been found by local residents and treasure hunters such as Larry Campbell from Montana. Residents have assumed that these represent the loot from coin machine burglaries that was tossed over the bridge when pursuit was closing in on the thieves.

Padre Island, TX – Hobbyists have tried over the years to search swimming beaches along this vast barrier island. Randy Nufeld of San Diego, CA, used a sluicebox device with a jet tube to process huge amounts of beach sand effectively.

Rosarita Beach, Baja California, Mexico – You're generally on your own in a foreign country such as this, but dredgers recovered hundreds of dollars in coins in this area between Ensenada and Tiajuana plus considerable jewelry until Mexican authorities stopped operations.

Southeastern U.S. – Numerous dredge operators work popular locations along the mouths of bayous and other streams, mostly looking for relics, but they find some coins. Larger relics are sucked from mud into the dredge nozzle and removed by hand. Most of the successful operators research the probable location of the routes of Civil War and Prohibition "blockade runners" and search accordingly.

Old Town, FL – Dredgers probing an old boat landing on the Suwanee River have found coins and jewelry in pockets in the muck along the sides of the stream. This is generally a muddy area, however, which inhibits any search.

Chapter 13

Knowing, Finding & Keeping Track

Three important aspects of coin hunting as a hobby are *knowing, finding and keeping track.* "Knowing" is the most interesting facet of the hobby; "finding" is by far the most thrilling; and "keeping track" can be the most satisfying as you accumulate and exhibit your collection.

How well do you know your coins? Do you know what they are actually worth on today's market? Do you know their history? These are just two examples of how "knowing" can be the most interesting aspect of coin hunting and collection. There are numerous books on the specific subjects of old coins, their histories and their values. Of course, these values change, and you'll need to develop numismatic sources that can let you keep up with these.

You may feel that the thrill has gone out of coin hunting for you after you have found several hundred coins . . . most of them worth only their face value. What's another penny, you probably ask yourself. When you dig up an old coin or some sort of special coin or token – whose value (larger than face value) you *know* from your studies . . . well, you'll find the thrill to be greater than ever!

Lastly comes what I identified as the most *satisfying* aspect of the hobby. How can keeping records be satisfying, you might be asking. Once you begin to see your collection grow . . . your coin albums and containers filling up . . . you will realize what a satisfying hobby this can be.

Finding Is Fun

Of course, there are many experienced and fine individuals

who have assembled impressive coin collections by various means . . . purchase, trade, inheritance and the like. You may wonder how you can "compete" with them. Yet your collection will always be "different," because you *found* the coins in it with your own sweat, patience and imagination. Becoming a well-rounded coin collector enables you to "finish off" the hobby properly. If you haven't begun to study coins and to learn their values, you should start immediately. Go to any library or coin collector's shop and look around at the books and other research materials available. Choose what you need to begin your personal collection and gain a real knowledge of numismatics – as opposed to just knowing what makes your detector sing out!

You'll learn the history of coins. People have been using them since about 650 B.C. The first coins were struck in Asia Minor, the cradle of civilization. They were bean-shaped lumps of gold, crudely stamped with a punch mark. Soon after, in Greece and Rome, coins flowered into things of beauty and fascinating historical interest. Since then, the various peoples of the world have designed, made and distributed unknown trillions of coins, medallions, trade and tax tokens and the like. Coin study is a world all its own, and an individual could spend a lifetime (some do!) just studying and collecting coins and related items.

When you study coins, you'll come to understand why people collect them . . . just as they collect such works of art as paintings and sculpture. After all, coins are miniature works of art, tiny bas relief sculptures designed by some of the world's greatest artists. Each coin has a story behind it . . . a tale of the triumphs and trials of a person, a country, a philosophy or a religion at some exciting or crucial time in the history of mankind. Each coin has a rich heritage and brings a wealth of pleasure and information to the collector.

There are many intriguing branches of numismatics with which you will suddenly find yourself involved as a coin hunter. Not only will you discover numerous different types of coins, both American and foreign, but you will dig up trade tokens, commemorative medallions, military decorations, tax tokens, convention badges, political campaign buttons and many other examples of man's creativity in media of exchange.

Tokens

Unless you've lived in a big city whose public transportation system required them, you've probably never thought about the abundance of tokens in our society . . . especially in the past. When the first sales taxes were enacted by the states, the value of a dollar was much greater than it is today and the actual amounts of sales were, therefore, far less than those of the present. To collect sales taxes properly; i.e. in fractions of a cent, it was necessary for states to mint tokens in these fractional denominations.

In my youthful days as a coin hunter these tokens were far more prevalent than they are as we approach the close of the 20th century. After all, the days of the Great Depression when tokens were so commonplace is now a half-century in the past! Still, you'll sometimes find tokens, and they should remind you of the Depression and one successful government effort to raise

In this photo from years ago, the Garrett family is shown recovering the hundreds of Colorado tax tokens shown at the upper left. The complete story is told in this chapter.

revenues in the midst of it. Some tax tokens were minted in quantities of thirty million pieces, but they have value today to collectors.

Most of all, tax tokens are fun to find and keep because they are souvenirs of the Great Depression and the years immediately following it into World War II. They are also among the last script issues of the various states. With each tax token you find remember that you have just recovered one of the last pieces of unique American memorabilia of an era gone by.

During a trip years ago my family and I chanced upon a spot where someone had dumped several hundred two-cent Colorado tax tokens. I was walking along a fence row seeking the site of a ghost town when I spied one of the tokens lying on the ground. Nudging the earth with my foot unearthed several more. My wife and children joined me at the spot where they too found these little metal objects. Then, my friend Hardrock Hendricks and his wife, with whom we had been seeking the ghost town site, joined our search party. After about an hour of sifting we determined that we had recovered all in that spot . . . a grand total of more than 300! Most were stamped from metal; some were round, and some were square. A few were stamped from some type of red rubber-like fiber. Why were all these tokens at this isolated spot? Your guess is as good as mine . . . and such "guessing" is one of the pleasures of treasure hunting!

Another interesting branch of numismatics is concerned with the extensive series of American tokens issued during the Civil War. They were about the size of today's penny and answered the demands of merchants for small change which had become scarce, as "hard money" was hoarded during the emergency. Tokens were either patriotic in theme or carried the name and address of the merchant who issued them, plus his advertising message.

Such tokens offer an intimate look at colorful slogans and patriotic sentiments, as well as the art work of the Civil War period. Indians in feathered headdresses, liberty heads, Washington, Lincoln, Jackson, Stephen Douglas and Gen. McClellan appear on the tokens, coupled with such patriotic sentiments as "The Union shall and must be saved," "The Flag of our Union. If anybody attempts to tear it down, shoot him on the spot," and

"No compromise with traitors." Others carry such private-interest propaganda as "Millions for contractors; not one cent for widows." Some merely state, "Exchange for one cent" or the simplistic "I owe you one cent."

Foreign Coins

You'll be completely amazed at the number of foreign coins you will find. How did they ever get here, you will ask. Most numerous, of course, will be Canadian and Mexican coins. European coins are quite common also, perhaps because of the tremendous quantities brought back by soldiers after the World Wars. These coins were generally given to children and, of course, lost. You may occasionally have the thrill of finding a foreign coin dated in the 11th or 12th century. This thrill will be short-lived when you discover the dating was based on the Mohammedan calendar not our Christian dating. Upon conversion your date in the 11th or 12th century becomes one in the 19th or 20th century.

As you search for coins you will also locate commemorative medallions. They date back to Roman times, and they have been issued since to celebrate important events of the day (or events that political leaders tried to make important). Medallions have been created in honor of famous people, events, animals and legends. Most of them were beautiful works of art when first made. Of course, medallions and special coins are still being manufactured. You'll find those that feature animals, artists, historic battles, presidents, military leaders, entertainers and many other subjects.

Try to learn the history behind each medallion that you find. This knowledge will be rewarding no matter what value can be placed on your finds. Of course, the medallions do not have the ready market value of coins, but you may be surprised at the interest collectors show in them.

Of course, your largest and most important collections will be of those United States coins that were minted in large quantities for general circulation. You'll be kept busy sorting and grading as you continuously add to and upgrade this collection. Inexpensive albums are available for most of the coin types that you will find. You'll probably want to start with the most recently dated penny, nickel, dime and quarter albums. Your interest and enthusiasm for coin hunting and collecting will grow as you watch these albums fill up.

This interest will spur you to get out on weekends to search the older and better coin hunting locations. Always keep your albums current. When you find a coin that can be graded better than the coin already filling a slot in your album, place the more valuable coin in the album. Keep all loose coins grouped according to dates and mint marks. Inexpensive plastic holders are available, or you can use the paper coin holders available from banks.

In addition to the fact that coin collecting will stimulate your interest in finding coins with a metal detector, a carefully planned collection will grow in value over the years, bringing increased profits. One of the great joys of coin collecting has to be the possession of knowledge that something you found or something that might come your way has real dollar value. While most of your coin finds will involve those of nominal value, you can honestly expect to discover a rare coin occasionally. It all depends on your efforts at research and the diligence of your actual scanning!

Of course, gold coins are the grand prizes of coin hunting and coin collecting. It's amazing to realize that such precious objects are still being found continually. Scarcely a week passes that I don't have a letter or picture from some coin hunter reporting news of a gold coin discovered with a Garrett detector. You, too, can find gold coins, but you must search *where they can be found.* In old communities and ghost towns, for example, seek out the mercantile establishments where "big money" transactions might have taken place. How do you find gold coins? This is a question I am continually asked. My reply is always the same. "First, must come research!"

Cultivate the friendship of other collectors or groups of coin hunters so that you can buy, sell and swap coins. Most cities with a population of more than few thousand have at least one coin dealer, whom you can locate through the Yellow Pages or other directories. Dealers generally are glad to appraise the value of a single coin at no charge, but it may be necessary to pay for the appraisal of a large collection.

Dealers provide you financial liquidity since coins may be sold to or through them at just about any time. In addition to local dealers you will find many others who advertise in hobby and coin publications. No matter what you see in an advertisement, never send coins unsolicited to any dealer. Always ascertain his interest first. Most coins shops have "bid boards" to which coins in plastic cases are sometimes affixed. Interested buyers will then bid on these coins, with the shop owner charging a percentage of the sale price.

To begin your coin collecting hobby go to a library. Read and study the books that interest you. Obtain the most current books with prices and investigate popular magazines of the hobby. If you're really interested, you'll want to subscribe to one of the industry bibles. They are *Coin World* and *Numismatic*

George Banks displays the $20 gold piece whose recovery with a Garrett detector is described here. Privately minted in 1855, its value is now hundreds of thousands of dollars.

News, both weeklies, and *Coin Age* and *Coins* Magazine, month-lies. They circulate within the industry, and the prices they list are for the trade.

Coin Dealers

Another way to immerse yourself in this hobby is to visit a coin dealer's shop and talk with him. Ask his advice about what you should read. Of course, any coin dealer is probably most concerned with making a sale to you, but you'll be surprised how many of them are hobbyists at heart, eager to share their experience.

Never trade or sell a coin without knowing its value. The mag-azines listed above are good current guides . . . but only if you have the latest issues. Inflation and the tastes and whims of col-lectors can cause these prices to vary widely. In earlier editions of this book I printed the prices of some coins to illustrate that they could range well up into the hundreds of thousands of dol-lars. Because these prices can fluctuate so widely (mostly upward!) I print few prices in this book. They might have changed drastically, even while we were printing it! Take my word. The prices paid for certain coins can be very high. Check for yourself at a coin dealer's shop or the coin trade publications.

Look at the photograph of the man holding the $20 gold piece that accompanies this chapter. Found with a Garrett detector more than 10 years ago at an old race track in the State of Wash-ington, this coin was then estimated to be worth $300,000. It was minted in 1855 in Sacramento, CA.

Above
Tiny, beautiful and valuable are the descriptive adjectives for this handsome gold coin that a hob-byist found with a Garrett metal detector.
Below
Impressive coin collections have been amassed in many ways, but the detector hobbyist always feels a personal sense of "discovery" with found coins.

The highest price ever brought by a single coin was the $725,000 paid in 1979 by a Chicago dealer for a privately minted Brasher Doubloon, named after a jeweler, Efraim Brasher, who designed the coin. Just recently MTB Banking Corporation paid $660,000 for another gold coin, an 1861 American "paquet reverse" Double Eagle, so rare that its single mate is in the Smithsonian in Washington.

When you find valuable coins, take care of them. Protect your property by keeping your coins in a safe place. Stories of thievery abound among collectors since there is such a ready market for coins. Because of this fact, it has also been suggested that you keep a record of the "peculiarities" of any especially valuable coins in your collection. Then, if one of them is stolen, you can immediately circulate its discription to collectors who will be on the lookout for it.

Make a note of the date, denomination and other numismatic characteristics of the coin, plus identifying features such as "scratch across the face," "nick on the edge," "hole drilled at the top," "diemark running through date," etc. This type of identification of your coins, kept in a safe place, could mean the difference between getting one of them back again if it is ever stolen . . . or never seeing it again.

There are so many things to consider if you want to get the most from your hobbies of coin hunting and collecting! You will learn as you progress how the knowing, finding and keeping-track tie the two hobbies together. Don't delay . . . get started doing this today!

The thrill that comes from finding just a plain, ordinary modern coin . . . one that might have been spent last week . . . is great. Just think of the thrill that would come from recovering a gold coin or one of the really rare silver ones. Keep searching! Just the possibility of discovering valuable coins should keep you working.

Hobbyist in England compares the coins recovered in a cache against published descriptions to determine the precise value of all that were discovered.

Chapter 14

Rules & Laws

This chapter is by no means intended to offer legal advice. In fact, I've always believed that the best advice you can give anyone who believes that he really has a legal problem is, "See a lawyer." This chapter, instead, will seek to raise just a few legal points that you should consider before going out into the field to hunt coins with your metal detector:

Ownership—Make every effort to return any piece of property that you find to its rightful owner. Now, I realize that there's no proof of ownership with a coin, but your metal detector is going to find other kinds of treasure, whether you want it to or not. And, you're probably looking forward to all the different kinds of things you will find.

Class rings, for example, sometimes have the name or initials of the owner engraved. They certainly have the name of the school from which he or she graduated and the year. These simple facts can often lead you into a fascinating puzzle with a most happy outcome when you return the ring. You might even find yourself with a reward or some flattering publicity! Such publicity can be valuable since it spotlights you as a person who can find lost jewelry and other metallic items with a detector. People may seek you out and offer to pay for your services. Honesty and a sincere respect for the property of others should govern the activities of every coin hunter.

Local regulations — Make certain that you are aware of them, especially in parks and similar regulated vacation and recreation spots. We've heard of equipment actually being confiscated when it was used illegally. And, remember, that ignorance of the law is no excuse! Ask those in authority, and when special permission is required, get it in writing.

"Destruction" of property — You'll learn that most every governmental subdivision – be it city, township, county, state or whatever – enforces some sort of law that prohibits the destruction of public or private property. When you dig a hole or cut through the grass on private or public property, you're in effect violating a law. Of course, laws are generally not enforced this rigidly, especially if the coin hunter is careful in his digging and retrieving. An experienced coin hunter seeks to leave an area that has been searched in such a condition that nobody will know that a metal detector has been in use there. I always urge hobbyists to leave any area they search in *better* condition than they found it!

Trespassing – *Don't*. It's that simple. Always heed "no trespassing" signs and never knowingly invade the property of others without getting permission. In some areas the very fact that you are trespassing voids your claim to any part of treasure that you might discover, regardless of other laws governing its ownership.

Ownership of Property

Finder's Keepers – There may be some truth in this old statement, especially about coins. But, there are certainly exceptions, particularly when you start considering other objects whose ownership can be more easily identified. No matter what kind of treasure you are looking for, I urge you to have a general knowledge of the laws of ownership. You can never tell what you'll find or where you'll find it! Finder's Keepers may not be appropriate for an object you discover on private or posted property if the landowner decides to dispute your claim. On the other hand, Finder's Keepers generally applies to any owner-not-identified item you find when you are not trespassing, when you are hunting legally on any public land and when the rightful owner cannot be identified. Of course, anyone can claim ownership of anything you find; it may then be left to the courts to decide the rightful owner.

Treasure Trove – In the United States this is broadly defined as any gold or silver in coin, plate or bullion and paper currency that has been found concealed in the earth or in a house belonging to another person, even when found hidden in movable property belonging to others such as a book, bureau, safe or a piece of machinery. To be classed as treasure trove the item(s) must have been lost long enough to indicate that the original owner is dead or unknown. All found property can generally be separated into five legal categories:

Abandoned property, as a general rule, is a tangible asset that has been discarded or abandonded wilfully and intentionally by its original owners. Thus, it becomes the property of the first person who discovers and desires it. An example would be a household item such as an appliance discarded into a trash receptacle. If the trash collector (or anyone else, for that matter) decides to take the appliance, they can do so legally.

Concealed property is tangible property hidden by its owners to prevent observation, inventory, acquisition or possession by other parties. In most cases, when such property found, the courts order its return to the original owner. Sometimes the

Nothing can escape a metal detector! Treasure hunters found these World War II military relics in California near desert camps used by General Patton for African training in 1942.

finder is given a small reward, more for his honesty in reporting the find than for the effort of discovery.

Lost property is defined as that which the owner has inadvertently and unintentionally lost yet to which he legally retains title. Still, there is a presumption of abandonment until the owner appears and claims such property, providing that the finder has taken steps to notify the owner of its discovery. Such a case might arise when someone finds a lost wallet that contains documents identifying the owner. It is the general rule that such property must be returned to its owner, who pays a reward if he so desires In fact, in almost every jurisdiction a criminal statute exists that makes it a crime to withhold "lost" property.

Misplaced property has been intentionally hidden or laid away by its owner who planned to retrieve it at a later date but forgot about the property or where it was hidden. When found, such property is generally treated the same as concealed property with attempts necessary to find its owner. When this is not possible, ownership of the property usually reverts to the occupant or owner of the premises on which it was found with the finder being awarded some amount of the object's value.

Things embedded in the soil generally constitute property other than treasure trove, such as antique bottles or artifacts of historical value. The finder acquires no rights to the object, and possession of such objects belongs to the landowner unless declared otherwise by a court of law. Generally, courts divide the value of the find between the property owner and the finder.

Finally, don't forget *income taxes* – federal, state and local. Monetary gain from coins or any treasure that you find must be declared as income in the year that it is received; that is, when you *sell* or spend the coins, not when you *find* them. Applicable expenses can be charged against the gain from any treasure discovered. Simply stated, however, tax laws require declaration of all income from treasure hunting. It is good, therefore, to keep complete and accurate records of what you spent for the equipment used in coin hunting and what additional expenses you incurred such as gasoline and other travel outlays.

Here's a suggestion on how to help *prove* that you're a professional treasure hunter. Have some cards printed. Yes, that's right . . . those business cards with your name address and telephone number . . . that we discussed in an earlier chapter. You might even advertise your services with a metal detector to help find lost items. Pass these cards out as you travel and give quantities to local jewelers and insurance agents. Place the cards on bulletin boards in appropriate places.

Rules of Conduct

Of course, the first rule of conduct for any treasure hunter is to *fill all holes*. In addition, property should always be restored to the condition in which you found it. I have heard of treasure hunters who completely devastate an area, leaving large gaping holes, tearing down structures and uprooting shrubbery and sidewalks. Damage of this kind is one of the reasons we're seeing so many efforts at legislation that would literally *shut down* metal detectors on public property.

Of course, there have always been laws to protect private as well as public property, but only in recent years have these been rigidly enforced to limit the activity of metal detector hobbyists.

Two treasure hunters visit the Garrett Museum to examine all of the many objects displayed that were discovered by metal detectors. Here, they are looking at some Roman coins.

Why has this happened? Public lands, parks, recreational areas and such are continuously maintained and kept in good condition so that those using such facilities can enjoy them to the fullest. When there is wilfull destruction, laws protecting the property are more rigidly enforced and new laws are sought. In Chapter 11 I discussed various methods you can use to retrieve coins and other objects without destroying landscaping and making unsightly messes.

Code of Ethics

Filling holes and protecting the landscaping is but one requirement of a dedicated metal detector hobbyist. Thousands of individuals and organization have adopted a formal Metal Detector Operators Code of Ethics:

"– I will respect private and public property, all historical and archaeological sites and will do no metal detecting on these lands without proper permission.

"– I will keep informed on and obey all laws, regulations and rules governing federal, state and local public lands.

"– I will aid law enforcement officials whenever possible.

"– I will cause no wilful damage to property of any kind, including fences, signs and buildings, and will always fill holes I dig.

"– I will not destroy property, buildings or the remains of ghost towns and other deserted structures.

"– I will not leave litter or uncovered items lying around. I will carry all trash and dug targets with me when I leave each search area.

"– I will observe the Golden Rule, using good outdoor manners and conducting myself at all times in a manner that will add to the stature and public image of all people engaged in the field of metal detection."

Policing this code is an important job of the scores of local metal detector and treasure hunting clubs organized over the nation. Clubs varying in size from a few members to hundreds meet regularly for fellowship, to share adventures and to compare their success in the field and water. At the same time, these sincere hobbyists seek knowledge of new developments in the science of metal detecting and try to remain abreast of the rapidly changing laws and regulations that govern their hobby. I believe that almost every hobbyist – especially one just learning about metal detectors – can benefit from membership in a club. This subject of clubs is discussed at greater length in the final chapter of this book.

Chapter 15
Cleaning Finds

I n most cases it is advisable to make no attempt to clean coins, other than to remove surface dirt with just a general light soaking in mild, soapy water. Do not use harsh dishwasher detergent; use only liquid hand soap. The slightest damage to a coin can degrade its numismatic value. Coin collectors prefer to buy coins as they are found and do their own cleaning rather than have someone attempt to clean a coin and destroy its value.

Of course, some of the coins you will find are quite dirty. And, none of us wants to carry a sack of dirty coins to the bank and ask for them to be exchanged for crisp new bills. So . . . remember that collectible coins should never be cleaned except by experts, but . . . if you must clean circulating coins, let's examine some of the ways.

Electrolysis

One of the most sophisticated means of cleaning is through the use of electrolysis. There are several electrolytic cleaners on the market, and one seems to work as well as the next. All operate on the principle of the removal of a tiny portion of the coin's metallic surface by sending a small electric current through the coin while it is submerged in a solution of water and citric acid. Generally a small glass about the size of an 8-oz cup is used with a stainless steel electrode similar to a tongue depressor submerged in the water.

One terminal of a low voltage (3 to 6v) supply is applied to this electrode in the water. The circuit is then completed when the other terminal is attached to the coin by means of an alligator clip or some spring tension device. A direct current of 10 to 100 mils is generally passed through the coin. The higher the current, the faster the surface metal will be removed from the coin. The metal, as it is removed, breaks up the surface corrosion. Coins are usually left in the bath from one to about 10 minutes. Following the electrolysis bath, the coins must be scrubbed with a small, soft brush.

This technique of electrolysis works quite well on some coins. It offers the opportunity for *permanent damage* to your coins, however, unless great care is taken in keeping the liquid either clean or separated for the different types of coins. Nickels should be cleaned in their own bath, pennies in their own bath and silver coins in still a third bath. Otherwise, nickels and dimes cleaned in a penny solution will turn red. The multi-clad coins which are growing in popularity can create similar problems. Coin cleaners of the electrolytic type are generally used on very badly corroded coins such as those which have been submerged in salt water for a long time.

Liquid Cleaners

I guess I've tried just about every type of liquid there is that claims to clean metal (and some that claim to clean other things). This has included the expensive solutions used by professional jewelers. Frankly, these high-priced solutions worked the best of all, but they leave a peculiar odor . . . and they are quite expensive. All things considered, my favorite cleaning liquids are either olive oil or a solution of white vinegar and salt.

When coins are soaked in olive oil anywhere from an hour to several days, surface corrosion will be loosened sufficiently so that a small brush will complete the cleaning process. I recommend that you use a small brush with fine wire to remove stubborn corrosion. Now, let me warn you. The olive oil will cause absolutely no harm, but you can scratch your coins with the wire brush, depending upon how hard you brush and for what length of time.

My recommendation for a cleaning method would be to use the white vinegar and salt solution, followed by a very light brushing, if necessary. Then, to protect your coin, wrap it in aluminum foil or place it in a tarnish-proof coin envelope.

When using the vinegar/salt method, you'll need separate glasses for copper and silver/nickel coins, primarily to avoid staining the dimes, nickels and quarters a copper color. To mix your solution pour one teaspoonful of table salt into each glass and add one ounce of white vinegar.

This solution will generally clean about six to eight coins at a time, and can be doubled for a quantity job. But, you've got to watch the coins pretty closely to get them in and out of the solution. Because some coins will be ready to remove before others, you shouldn't be try to watch too many at the same time. Some coins will clean faster and easier than others, but you can help things along by rubbing them with your fingers and dropping them back into the cleaner. A few coins may need to stay here for as long as an hour, but most will come clean in seconds or minutes. Your coins will turn dull if left too long in the solution. Of course, this dull finish will not harm their monetary value, and it won't be as unsightly as the tarnish. Quite frankly, however, I believe you can do the best job of cleaning your coins if you will rinse them at the proper time.

Your rinse container should be filled with cold water and left under a slowly running tap. When the coins begin to shine brightly in the vinegar/salt bath, transfer them to the rinse.

This portion of a silver cache discovered with a metal detector shows pieces of the precious metal were crudely minted and cut to produce "homemade" cobs for trading pieces.

After the coins have rinsed for about three minutes, you can wipe them or spread them out on a towel to dry.

This method is essentially for coins that are merely tarnished. Those that are badly encrusted will have to be scrubbed with a brush as described above.

When to Clean

It is advisable that you make no cleaning effort in the field; that is, starting to clean coins as soon as they are recovered. In trying to rub the coin clean or remove dirt from it while you're still hunting, you may scratch or mar its surface. Plus, cleaning coins takes time away from your coin hunting . . . the reason you're out in the field!

When you return from hunting, place those coins that need cleaning in a wooden or plastic bowl. Handle them gently and use a mild, soapy solution . . . no harsh detergents or powders. Try to separate the coins so that one does not lie on top of another. After they have soaked for a while, gently rub each with a soft cloth to remove most dirt and contamination. Only then can you behold the beauty of your discoveries.

And, aren't they *beautiful!*

Still, when you determine that additional cleaning is required, you can clean the circulating coins by one of the other methods described in this chapter or some other technique that you have devised. For your valuable finds . . . and, even the finds that you *suspect* are valuable, I urge you to let them be cleaned by a specialist. Don't take the chance of reducing any coin's value by damaging it through improper cleaning. The money you lose will be your own!

Keep in mind, also, that it is seldom advisable to clean any coin beyond the mild soaking and light rubbing. When you become acquainted with coin dealers, you will learn that they would rather buy coins that have not been cleaned, except to remove loose surface contamination. Dealers seem to prefer coins with the natural, aged look. I agree because to me coins that retain the normal colors after they have been in the ground for a period of time are far more beautiful than coins that have been made shiny or streaked by poor cleaning attempts. The patinas supplied by Mother Nature are far more beautiful than any that can be devised by Man.

Iron Relics

Frequently, the coin hunter will discover a valuable iron relic of one sort or another, such as a cannon or musket ball. If the relics have been buried for many years (since the Civil War!) or if they have been buried in mineralized or corrosive soils (the beach, for example), they could be not only heavily rusted but well on their way to disintegration.

So, when you retrieve an iron relic . . . when you dig it up out of the ground in a heavily rusted condition, understand that exposure to air will cause it to continue to deteriorate, even after you have thoroughly cleaned it. For short-term preservation, pop the item into a bucket of water. If you want to preserve an iron object indefinitely, paint it with a coating of polyurethane varnish. The varnish will stop air from reaching the surface and prevent further rusting and deterioration.

Finally, before leaving this subject of cleaning, let me caution you that if you find jewelry which has imitation or paste stones, do not try to clean it beyond soaking in a mild, soapy solution. Also, in cleaning jewelry, be extremely careful with items that feature mounted pearls, opals, turquoise and coral. And, remember that mountings can *rust*. Be careful how you handle any jewelry with mounted stones, especially in the field when the piece is dirty and you can't examine it very well. Just assume that the mountings are rusting and that the jewels are about to fall out. Then, handle accordingly!

Always remember that cleanliness may be healthy for your body and soul, but it's not especially good for old coins. Be careful how you clean the ones that you find!

Good healthy exercise and plenty of sunshine in the great outdoors are simple benefits enjoyed by every hobbyist who participates in hunting coins.

Chapter 16

Your Good Health

The major beneits to be derived from coin hunting, I have come to believe, concern the *health* of the hobbyist . . . mental as well as physical! Good exercise outdoors in the fresh air . . . exercise that is sustained but not overly strenuous . . . exercise under the absolute control of the individual, if you will . . . benefits men and women, girls and boys, of all ages. And, the zest and thrill that the hobby brings are an absolute joy to the soul. There's no "time limit" to coin hunting, and a hobbyist is never forced to "keep up" with a younger or more athletic or experienced competitor. Anybody can hunt for coins for hours a day or for just a short while; the hunting may be intense or involve little exertion.

Hunting for coins with a metal detector is an ideal hobby for young people, full of energy and curiosity, with a desire for adventure and excitement. The hobby is perhaps even more suitable for mature men and women . . . yes, senior citizens, whose health permits (or requires) light outdoor exercise and who have maintained their spirit of adventure.

People of all ages and in all stages of physical condition enjoy the hobby of hunting for coins with a metal detector. They roam parks and beaches, and they wade into the surf and swimming areas as they look for coins. You'll also find hobbyists in ghost towns and in gold mining areas in search of treasure. For the most part, these people are active and dynamic. They're enthu-

Note the erect stance and outstretched arm of this hobbyist which permits him to cover maximum area yet search for hours without straining any muscles.

siastic about what they are doing. And, few generally spend much time worrying about their body or their health.

As a result, some coin hunters occasionally complain of muscle pains or aching joints after they have used a metal detector for long periods of time. It's been my experience that most such complaints come from newcomers to the hobby who have become captivated by it. They've made their first discovery or found their first *good* coin and can't get enough of metal detecting. As a result, they swing the detector 10 or 12 hours those first days. And, they stoop over and dig a lot!

The following morning they naturally wake up with a good case of cramped muscles and maybe a sore joint or two. After a short time, the soreness either disappears or is eased out of the mind by the memory of yesterday's finds. And, off they go again! Oftentimes, that first discovery of another good coin proves to a better dose of medicine than any salve or liniment!

Incidentally, don't laugh at the behavior of novices. I've heard of plenty of veteran coin hunters who go through the same experience on the first good day outside after a long winter!

In some of my earlier books I have offered the following suggestions for lessening the danger of strained muscles:

– Select the *proper equipment,* including accessories, considering weight and balance in relation to your general physique and level of stamina.

– Strengthen hand, arm, back and shoulder muscles through a moderate *exercise* program;

– Before beginning each day's detecting activity, spend a few minutes *warming up* with simple, easy stretching exercises;

– During the actual activity of metal detecting, use common sense in how you employ your muscles; use *correct scanning techniques* and take an occasional break.

Let's expand on proper scanning techniques. First, keep a firm footing at all times; never try to scan while standing on one foot or in some other unnatural position. Make all movements as natural as possible. If you find yourself scanning on steep hills, in gullies and other unlevel places, keep good balance, take shorter swings and don't let yourself get in an awkward position.

Grasp the metal detector handle lightly. If you've selected an instrument such as my Grand Master Hunter with light weight and excellent balance, you'll scarcely know you're holding a detector. Slight wrist and arm movements in scanning are necessary when you are moving the searchcoil from side to side in short swings. If you swing the detector widely, use a method that is natural and one that causes a minimum amount of unnecessary wrist movement. Let your entire arm "swing" with the detector. You'll also find handling a pistol-grip detector such as any of Garrett's Freedom models to be as easy as pointing a finger.

Occasionally, change hands and use the other arm to swing the detector. If you ever feel yourself tightening up, stop and rest. Most likely, however, you'll get enough rest just digging up the coins you find. Thus, getting a little rest becomes still another reason to find more coins! Also, stooping down and digging up a coin gives other muscles a workout, which will help prevent possible muscle soreness from swinging the detector for long periods without a break.

Most important of all, use common sense and take care of yourself! There are no "time limits" to metal detecting. You have the rest of your life.

When to Hunt

And, speaking of time . . . you may be asking . . . just when should I hunt? Is there a special time better than others? Time of day? Time of year?

The answer to all your questions is to hunt any time . . . day or night, morning or evening, rain or shine, summer or winter . . . all seasons are coin hunting seasons. Use your own best judgment and, always remember, you're hunting because you *want* to and because you enjoy it. If the hobby should ever become tedious or boring, give it a rest and wait for your interest to return. Frankly, I can't imagine that hunting for treasure could ever be *boring,* what with all the wonderful coins, items of jewelry and other valuable objects just waiting to be found.

But, when to hunt . . . here's a suggestion. After your evening meal, you might go to a nearby park or swimming area and search for an hour or so. On weekends you can spend up to full-time searching outlying and out-of-town sites. On vacations make it a habit to stop along the roadway at various parks and roadside stops where you and family can stretch your legs and refresh yourselves. At the same time, you can search and recover a coin or two lost by those folks who've used the park before you.

Hunting with a metal detector is a good way to limber up in the morning and get the blood circulating. Get up an hour earlier than normal; drive to the park or into the downtown area and search along heavily congested traffic areas. Get out before most people do; the rewards will be yours. If you work in an area close to a park or any location where people play or congregate, you can walk over to this area during your lunch break and hunt for half an hour or so. Any time you're driving along and see an area that looks promising . . . stop, get out with your detector and scan a sweep or two. You'll never know what you may find until your detector sings out and you dig!

Don't Get Stung!

The above warning does not concern buying a low quality or cheap detector . . . that is discussed elsewhere in this book! It's inevitable that people who venture into the out-of-doors are going to get bitten or stung by gnats, mosquitos, bees, ants, wasps, spiders, ticks, hornets, scorpions or other such ugly creatures. Generally, all that results is a brief moment or so of slight discomfort or pain. But, the results can be deadly.

Since the coin hunter is out of doors, he should be aware of the dangers from insects and other varmints. Of course, the greatest danger from most of these is during the warm months of late spring, summer and early fall. There is very little danger during cold weather. To avoid insects, generally, it's good idea not to use scented preparations such as deodorants, hair spray and perfume which might tend to attract them. If you're in an unknown area or one where you've been bothered by insects before, keep a can of insecticide handy. If you are allergic to stings, be certain to follow your doctor's advice.

The bite of a spider can be very dangerous, and that of a scorpion will be *very* painful. So, be especially alert for them. You're most likely to find spiders around old buildings, old lumber, dump grounds and trash areas. They might also be in old houses or areas that have not been disturbed for some time. Scorpions can be found in warmer climates. To avoid spiders, scorpions and similar creatures, always be careful where you put your hands and feet. It's been 12 years since I've even *seen* a scorpion, so you have little to fear if you just watch your step and where you place your hands.

Use good common sense. Wear sturdy gloves when moving debris and lumber. Look on the underside of lumber and other large objects *before* picking it up, whenever possible. Don't get under old buildings or porches unless you proceed cautiously. You might want to consider wearing a hat or scarf to keep insects out of your hair, especially when searching in or under an old structure. Always carefully inspect any areas before you enter them. Ticks and chiggers (in Texas, for sure!) give some of us real fits. Their season starts in March or April and ends in September, with the peak coming in the hottest months. Of course, fire ants in many places have devoured most ticks, but it seems ants are now more of a problem than ticks used to be!

I'm certainly not trying to *scare* you with all this talk about insects and such. But, it's a good idea to keep them in mind *any* time you're out of doors. As I said earlier, use your good common sense, and you'll be fine!

Chapter 17
Tips from Readers

E ver since I first began writing articles and books about coin hunting, tips on the hobby have been given to me by customers and friends. Come to think of it . . . I received these tips even *before* starting to publish my work. In the early days of Garrett Electronics, when I would speak at a seminar, some of those attending would come up afterwards and share their ideas with me. Of course, many of them would also ask for a *copy* of my talk . . . and, that's how I got into the writing business!

But, in this chapter of the new book, I want to share with you some of the ideas that have been so freely given to me.

J. B. Estes suggests that you always scan the backbone of books. (You can use a pocket scanner . . . see Chapter 18.) He does this at all flea markets and garage sales he attends. He says that many people hide coins in the backbone of hardcover books. He reports finding several coins this way, two of which were gold coins. J.B. also suggests that you search around fireplaces for coins that might be hidden between fireplace bricks, possibly by children.

Harry & Lucille Bowen report good results searching around baptismal areas of old churches, faucets in parks, bases of old trees (where coats might once have been thrown) and "whisky rocks" from Prohibition days. (Now, I didn't know what a whisky rock was, either; so, I asked.) Seems that during Prohibition, peddlers of bootleg hootch would designate certain places, such as a rock or tree stump, where they would make deliveries and exchange liquor for money that was left there. I understand that this was also a common practice near construction gangs who were not allowed to take booze on the job. As a last suggestion from the Bowens, check with your city engineer's office to locate places that are to be or have been demolished. All such condemned areas and areas of excavation make good coin hunting sites.

Specialize

Perhaps in addition to your general coin hunting you may want to specialize in searching certain types of areas such as fairgrounds, parks, old circus grounds, ghost towns, old church yards and the like.

Jim Watson of Greenville, TX, specialized in searching old settlers' campgrounds. From one such campground near Sherman, he retrieved more than 2,000 old coins, all dated between 1875 and 1925. The good thing about coin hunting in places like this is that all the coins will be old, he reports, because very few of the campgrounds that he searches are still in use.

Since Jerry Nunn of Charlotte, NC, has decided to specialize in *old* coins, he tries to hunt in church yards established in the last century or earlier. In a period of less than three years he found more than 2,000 coins in the yards of old churches in Maryland and North Carolina. His largest haul came at a one-room church just outside Washington, DC, where he found some 100 coins.

If you have a desire to specialize in certain coin hunting areas and locations, there is one simple way to choose the type of area in which you wish to specialize. Continue hunting for coins in various areas as you are now doing. The first time you find an area that is especially "hot" and contains many coins or old and valuable ones, consider that particular type of hunting site as your specialty. Some suggestions, in addition to those mentioned above, are old or abandoned drive-in theaters, old country stores, communities devasted by such disasters as fires, floods or tornados, natural springs, plus dozens of others too numerous to mention.

More Tips

Always check vending machine and telephone coin slots. Just use your fingers! You'll be amazed how many times you find coins that others have left behind.

Bob Barnes of Oklahoma recommends that city hunters

search the grassy areas adjacent to sidewalks and streets. He's found these areas to be good while many playgrounds have been "worked to death."

Dick Ferrick sent in another good tip. He said that he has been successful in finding coins and other pocket items under and around telephone and power poles and guy wires. Apparently, boys and girls play on and around these places; he knows for certain that they *lose coins* here!

This suggestion comes from W. G. Eslick who strongly encourages coin hunters to search and re-search all *known* coin producing areas. He says that with meticulous searching anyone will probably find coins in areas that have been worked many times before. This suggestion of Mr. Eslick is especially appropriate today with the new detectors coming out that search so much deeper and with such greater sensitivity. Inferior detectors of the past, poor scanning methods, varying soil conditions and other reasons have caused many, many coins to be overlooked. It can absolutely "boggle your mind" to think of all the coins that were simply *scanned over* by the older detectors

Author's late father shown searching yard of burned and abandoned church. Mr. Garrett's memory guided Charles and his two brothers on many treasure hunts with metal detectors.

because targets were too deep, were masked by a larger piece of trash or for some other reason. *Go get them!*

Never . . . repeat, *never* . . . neglect to search an area simply because you've been told that it's "already been gone over with a metal detector." When someone tells me that, I just laugh (sometimes to myself) and reply, "Well *I've* never searched it with *this* detector!"

Use a Rake

Joseph W. Gehrke has written to tell me how raking pays off for him. Using an ordinary garden rake he cleans off trashy areas before beginning to search with his detector. He says the raking not only eliminates a lot of metallic junk but helps him find valuable items on the surface and even gains him access to some areas. He was admitted to one ghost town in southern Arizona that was strictly off limits to THers when he showed caretakers his rake and told them that he removed all debris and never left holes. This "volunteer yard cleaner" not only became friendly with the ladies in charge and left with many late 19th and early 20th century coins but has a standing invitation to return.

William and Donna Johnson suggest trying to determine "spill patterns" in your favorite coin hunting areas. For example, they have found that coins can most usually be found about 10 to 15 feet from the trunk of a large tree. They determined this fact by searching around trees in a strict grid pattern and keeping precise records. Why not try this in some of the locations where you hunt successfully? It might make your job easier when you discover the very same kind of location somewhere else.

Become Popular

Several hobbyists, including R.C. Mills of Jackson, TN, have suggested that you can find many doors (and the yards in front of them) opened to you when you hand out printed business cards to owners of houses or other buildings where you want to search. Some property owners will even alert you to other good locations. It's hard for a person not to respond to a card that says something like, "I search with a metal detector for lost coins, jewelry and other objects. I promise not to destroy any property, to leave no holes unfilled and to leave the area like I found it." A card like this can make you more popular!

J. R. Rowland of the Oregon Treasure Hunters League says you can also be more popular if you learn to *gid*. He explains that to retrieve coins, you generally have to *dig*. He suggests that

These coins were found with a metal detector by William and Donna Johnson in their "experiment" to determine the pattern of coins that were lost beneath an old school yard tree.

after you pocket your find, you do the reverse of "dig," which is, of course, *gid!* Fill those holes!

I love to search ghost towns which I consider one of the last frontiers of treasure hunting. There are so many magical things to find in them, and they're not generally searched very thoroughly. For one thing, a ghost town will probably be darned hard to find, and it won't be a place you can keep coming back to because it's so inconvenient to reach in the first place!.

In the Big Bend country of West Texas you'll find numerous ghost towns, some not too far off good roads. Whenever you can, ascertain ownership and get permission before you dig.

In a magazine article Dave Scott offered some good advice to all of us coin hunters. He recommended that we let trash be our friend. That's right, he believes that the trash so many of us rant and rave about is masking many good finds. New detectors with more sensitivity and better discrimination will permit searching those areas that have discouraged others because trash has camouflaged signals from coins. A small, Super Sniper search-

Chris Adams of Rochester, NY, displays coins and tokens he has found with a metal detector. Even black-and-white photography shows the varied patinas acquired by the coins.

coil will also let you search more effectively here.

Take old soda pop stands. The ground is literally paved with bottlecaps, but mixed among them can be found many coins. Dave suggests that you search for nooks and crannies around the caps and that you hunt at the perimeter of the junk . . . with a small searchcoil, of course.

You can combine Dave's "junk" idea with Joe Gehrke's rake and clean out some of the junk yourself. Of course, if you want to dig up a layer of bottle caps, always fill in the area to leave it in better condition than you found it. And, dispose properly of any junk you dig or rake up!

You'll find good ideas almost every month in one or more of the treasure magazines that report happenings of our hobby and stories about it. Also featured in these magazines are the advertisements of manufacturers. These let you keep up with new innovations in equipment . . . or, at least, what we manufacturers *report* as new innovations!

As I've stated many times before, you can never know *all there is* about coin hunting. I know that I don't. There are just too many good ideas that people are waiting to tell me about . . . in writing, in a magazine article or in person.

Chapter 18

Detectors & Searchcoils

Metal detectors for coin hunting come in all shapes and sizes . . . and prices. This chapter will try to provide an overview of the various kinds of detectors that are available. Once again, I must point out that we will consider only *quality* detectors, the type of instruments that you should *expect* to find coins for you.

How expensive should a metal detector be? There's a great deal of discussion that always goes on concerning the subject of price, and I certainly don't intend to avoid the subject. Of course, you must start out with a high quality metal detector. You should choose one especially designed for coin hunting or one of the universal instruments. A properly designed universal detector . . . one that can be used for hunting coins as well as caches, searching ghost towns and beaches, even prospecting . . . is going to be expensive and cost upwards of $600. But, it will be well worth it for a long-time career . . . in coin hunting, as well as for any other uses of a metal detector that you want to enjoy. And, believe me, as you progress in the hobby, you *will* want to hunt for other types of treasure!

You can expect to get a fine coin-hunting instrument for something under $500, and quality "beginner" detectors can run several hundred dollars less than that. I really hope that you will never make price your only criterion for judgment . . . whenever you buy a detector . . . and, no matter what brand you buy. The most expensive instrument may not be the best one for you. Work with a dealer you can trust; you'll enjoy relying on his judgment throughout thour career as a metal detector hobbyist.

Concerning price, let me strongly advise you not to buy "cheap" instruments (under $100, for example) so widely advertised. It's rule of mine never to *knock* the equipment of any metal detector manufacturer, but these so-called "detectors" hardly qualify as coin-finding equipment. Most of them are bothered by ground minerals and at best can detect coins only a fraction of the depth that better instruments can. A single missed coin could easily "pay" the amount you were trying to save. Too, when you know you're using a cheap detector, you'll always wonder what you're missing.

How to Buy

Carefully review the published data of all the major manufacturers and work with a dealer you respect and trust before selecting an instrument as best suited for your needs. I really suggest that you read my new and totally revised *Modern Metal Detectors*, which devotes one of its four major sections to this important subject. You might also get some ideas from the revised version of my old favorite for beginners, *Treasure Hunting Pays Off.*

Here's my recommendation...after completing all of the steps I've discussed, select the detector you want to purchase. Then, come up with another $50 or $100 so that you can buy a detector just a little better. That's right, buy an instrument that's one grade above the one that you intended to buy. You'll

Facing
Whatever is behind the stucco wall of this crumbling old house will not be able to hide from a good pocket scanner.

Over

Above
This Crossfire elliptical searchcoil is ideal for searching in tight places that will not accommodate a traditional coil.

Below
The ability to fit in tight, rocky places is but one of the advantages offered by elliptical coils and the 4 1/2-inch Super Sniper coil shown here.

have a superior detector, and you'll soon be glad you spent the extra money. Believe me!

Now to discuss metal detectors, generally. On most of the electronic metal detectors made by Garrett and other major manufacturers the control housing is mounted on one end of a stem with a searchcoil at the other. The cable connecting the searchcoil and control housing is wound around the stem, and the detector is carried by a handle either at the end of the stem or on the control housing. Many variations of this configuration can be seen, but some detectors are still as bulky and unwieldy as they were 30 years ago.

On the other hand, Garrett and other progressive manufacturers have devised exciting new designs for their modern metal detectors. Let's examine some of these configurations:

Standard

As noted above, the basic (or standard) configuration of most detectors features a control housing attached to the handle and stem with a cable wound around the stem to the searchcoil. This configuration is both historic and traditional and can be traced back to the earliest commercial models.

On such modern detectors as the Garrett Master Hunter series, however, comfort and ease of handling are of far more concern than custom or tradition. These detectors feature what is often called a "wrist action" model. You should always consider balance and weight of utmost importance in the selection of

Facing

Charles Garrett uses computers to design modern searchcoils scientifically to enhance all the specific features of his company's detectors.

Over

This coin hunter paid a relatively low price for his simple pistol-grip detector, but he relied on his dealer and the manufacturer's reputation.

a standard configuration detector. Newcomers to the hobby and veterans alike often want to spend long hours in the field with their detectors. An instrument that is heavy or improperly balanced can leave muscles sore and dispositions ruffled. On the other hand, lightweight models can be used for long periods with little physical or mental fatigue.

Recognizing the importance of light weight, Garrett years ago began using specially molded housings that were both lighter and more durable than the traditional "little tin box" housings once so popular. In addition, the new housings are more attractive when the detector is new and remain good looking for years. No longer must a coin hunter be embarrassed about the looks of a favorite old detector because its paint is scarred and its housing is dented!

Balance, too, is important in lessening strain on hand and arm muscles. We define balance as the ease with which a detector rests in the hand when held in the normal operating position with searchcoil extended. Little effort should be required to hold the searchcoil in the air at operating height. Light weight and good balance that is possible with a good wrist-action detector will result in minimal fatigue experienced both during and after treasure hunting.

Grand Master Hunters CX II and III and the Master Hunter CX, for example, are particularly well balanced. Just a single finger placed beneath the forward end of the handle permits any of these detectors to float perfectly in the air at the proper scan angle. The operator is not forced to raise the coil continually to keep it balanced. The detector's handle permits complete grip comfort. In fact, it is not necessary to "grip" the handle at all; simply let the detector float comfortably as it is cradled in the curled fingers of either hand.

The meter is placed in a protected position on the end of the handle for both visibility and rugged performance. Touchpads, the major controls of these particular instruments, are placed right at the hand of the operator where they can be reached easily and operated instantly by the touch of a thumbtip.

Pistol-Grip

As manufacturers sought to make their detectors easier to handle, the pistol-grip model was developed. This type of detector usually features a built-in extension arm rest as well as the easily grasped handle that furnishes its name. Excellent balance and light weight are both generally features of this type instrument. These enable a hobbyist to count on scanning for hours without tiring. The pistol-grip stem is designed both for hunting on land as well as in shallow water.

This type of detector can be moved about easily as the operator carries out scanning techniques. With the detector as an "extension" of the arm and hand, its searchcoil stem lies along the same line as the forearm. Motion is accomplished without thinking since operation is almost as simple as *pointing a finger.*

The new Garrett Ultra GTA detectors that achieved instant popularity as the world's most effective for coin hunting feature this pistol-grip design as do the popular Garrett Freedom detectors. Touchpads on every GTA detector as well as its unique *Graphic Target Analyzer™* are all on the front of the detector facing the operator. Easy access controls on each Freedom models are also within quick and easy reach.

Metal detectors can find coins of all ages and values. Literally priceless, these came from a group found in Greece with the two on the left dating from the period around 400 B.C.

Those Freedom models with pinpointing and other trigger controls place them at the operator's "trigger finger."

Pistol-grip configurations have proven quite popular for coin hunting. Such detectors are also designed for finding coins on the beach and in shallow surf. Light and easy to handle, they perform well in these areas provided that searchcoils have adequate environmental protection to be submersible.

Hip-Mount

This configuration features the control housing on a belt around the waist or slung over the shoulder with the searchcoil on an adjustable-length stem. An armrest is also usually supplied as an extension of the stem. Many standard detectors can be converted to this configuration designed to relieve the arm of weight. This model is ideal for those hobbyists who desire, for one reason or another, to minimize the weight that is carried by the hands and arms.

On any model that is to be worn on the hip, it is important that all controls be easily accessible in this configuration.

The use of the hip-mount configuration requires searchcoil cable that is considerably longer than that required for the wrist- action or pistol-grip configurations. Ninety inches is the normal length. If you purchase a detector and plan to use it mounted on your hip, make certain that the searchcoils you buy along with it have cables that are the proper length.

Using searchcoils with standard-length cable on a hip-mounted detector will require an extension cable two to three feet in length with mating conductors. Fitting out your detector in such a way offers no particular problem except in waterproofing. Make certain that your connectors are environmentally protected if they will be submerged or exposed to dampness.

Chest-Mount

These models, while quite functional, have never enjoyed very much popularity. Usually, the control housing is suspended with a cross-shoulder strap that holds the housing flat against the upper chest. This configuration is sometimes designed to try to protect the housing against submersion while the detector is being used in shallow water.

Use of such a configuration also permits men and women to enjoy the hobby even though they must bear any sizable weight with their back or upper body muscles.

When converting a detector to chest-mount configuration, make certain that all controls are easily accessible.

Flotation-Mounted

This configuration locates the control housing on a flotation device when the detector is used for hunting in calm water such as lakes, ponds or gentle surfs. The number and variety of such devices are limited only by the imagination of water hunters. As discussed in Chapter 12, I am not a particular fan of this configuration.

Underwater Designs

The Garrett Sea Hunter XL500 detector is manufactured for use in depths to 200 feet, which is generally a little deeper than most coin hunters want to go. Designed for efficient land, surf and underwater hunting, it is built in the hip-mount configuration but the control housing can also be mounted on an arm, leg or the upper chest. Of primary concern to many underwater hunters, however, is keeping such bulk from the body. Divers in "tight" situations such as shipwrecks do not want to be encumbered with large objects strapped to the body.

Garrett produces its "Scuba-Mate" for such divers. This accessory is a mobile underwater platform on which the detector is mounted. Only the headphone cord connects it to the diver. In any emergency, therefore, the rig can be scuttled easily. It can also be lowered to a diver, when necessary, so that swimming movements are not encumbered with this added weight.

Pocket Scanners

Garrett has only recently introduced its Pocket Probe hand-held detector. Yet, we are already hearing from many coin hunters about how one of the most effective tools in their bag of tricks can be the pocket scanner or so-called "hand-held" detector, still another configuration in which metal detecting equipment is designed and manufactured. Of course, all treasure hunting metal detectors are held in the hand, but pocket scanners can literally fit into an individual's palm.

These detectors obviously can penetrate to little depth, but they are very handy for the treasure hunter who is trying to search difficult places – particularly inside a house. You can quickly scan ceilings, walls and floors with such a detector. This little detector can scan in tight places where even the smallest searchcoil could not be used. A good example is the deep hole from which you've just removed a coin. When you retrieve a coin or any metallic object – valuable or not – from a hole, always scan over the hole to determine if additional metal objects are still buried there. There are many cases where more than one coin or more than one piece of jewelry has been retrieved from the same hole.

An effective pocket scanner should be a tool used by all modern coin hunters.

Searchcoils

Searchcoils are an integral – and vitally important – component of any modern metal detector. We urge that you never take your searchcoil for granted or overlook its importance. The finest detector in the world can be no better than its searchcoil.

It is obvious that no detector can operate without a searchcoil. What is not so obvious is that the type of searchcoil used with a modern detector will determine how effectively it will perform the task that has been assigned to it . . . indeed, how effectively it can perform *any* task. You wouldn't use cheap or retread tires on a high-speed motorcar. Don't expect an intricate modern detector to operate effectively with a low quality searchcoil.

You can depend upon a searchcoil made by any of the quality detector manufacturers. It just stands to reason that Garrett or any other manufacturer wants its detectors equipped with the searchcoils that enable that detector to perform best. This raises the question of searchcoils built by companies other than detector manufacturers . . . those that claim their coils will *improve* detector performance.

Well, I don't know much about those searchcoils. But, I do know a lot about the Crossfire searchcoils on Garrett detectors. In fact, I imagine I know *more* about Garrett equipment than anyone else, and I would expect the same to be true of the other quality manufacturers. If I believed that a *better* searchcoil could be built for one of my detectors, you can bet your life that I would build it and you would find it on a Garrett detector when you bought one.

Just what is a searchcoil? Let's continue our motorcar analogy and define it in automobile terms. Searchchoils basically have the same function as wheels on a car. Wheels take power from the motor and interface between the automobile and the ground. They roll along, take bumps and shocks to permit the car to perform its function of getting to a destination. Searchcoils take power from the control housing via the searchcoil cable. They are the interface between the metal detector and the ground. They take bumps and shocks as they scan to permit the detector

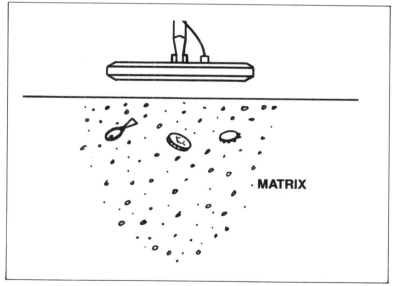

This typical matrix below a metal detector's searchcoil illustrates how the electromagnetic field generated from that searchcoil "illuminates" every metal target in the area below.

to perform its function of finding metal targets.

Most searchcoils operate with electromagnetic transmitter and receiver antennas embedded within the searchcoil. The searchcoil is mounted on the lower end of a stem to be scanned over bare ground or a specific object. An invisible electromagnetic field generated by the transmitter winding flows out into whatever medium is present – soil, rock, water, sand, wood, air or whatever. Further description of this process is given in Chapter 4.

Because design and construction of searchcoils is so critical, we manufacturers of modern metal detectors are quite concerned with it. Wire and plastic contract and expand with normal temperature changes, affecting the electrical parameters of searchcoils. Instability, drift and erratic operation will result unless extreme care has been exercised in the design and manufacture of the searchcoil.

An important aspect of any searchcoil is the effective scanning width it provides through the mounting of its antennas and other design criteria. Just because the shell of a searchcoil is eight inches in diameter does not mean that that coil will scan an eight-inch swath. I urge you to experiment. You may be amazed at the limitations of some detector searchcoils.

Also very important to coin hunters is the searchcoil's ability to pinpoint accurately. New detectors feature precise electronic pinpointing, with circuitry especially designed for such a purpose. Without the proper searchcoil, however, this special pinpointing circuitry is useless.

Searchcoils come in many shapes and sizes. Roughly speaking, the smaller the searchcoil, the smaller the object that can be detected. Larger searchcoils are primarily designed to detect larger, deeper targets, but they can locate tiny objects at great depths as well.

Environmental Protection

Effective searchcoils should offer some degree of environmental protection, primarily against rain and other forms of water. Even if a hobbyist doesn't intend to hunt coins in shallow water, searchcoils should be able to resist moisture that will occasionally be encountered. It might be well to review here the "waterproofing" designations in general use with searchcoils.

Splashproof indicates that operation will not be affected if a small amount of water gets on the searchcoil, such as moisture from wet grass. *Waterproof* means that the searchcoil can be operated in heavy rain with no danger from the moisture. *Submersible* indicates that a searchcoil can be submerged as deep as the cable connector without affecting the detector's operation.

Make certain you understand the water-resistant capabilities of your searchcoil. This is important! All Garrett searchcoils are fully submersible. That means that they can not only "resist moisture," but operate effectively when submerged in water to the connector and sustain no water damage. This may be not true of the searchcoil you are using. Make certain of its environmental integrity before you risk ruining it by dunking it in the water!

All searchcoils are not alike. They vary widely both in quality and in what they will enable a detector to find. Simply stated, a good searchcoil is vital to the success of a metal detector. No coin hunter should seek a "bargain" in purchasing a searchcoil!

Electronic Shielding

Searchcoils must also be electronically shielded to protect them from electrostatic interference. The most common type of such interference will probably come from wet grass. Most manufacturers shield the windings of modern searchcoils with what is called a Faraday Shield. Once again, however, we urge you not to take this protection for granted. Question before you purchase a searchcoil, or test it for yourself in this manner. With the audio threshold of your detector properly adjusted, drag a handful of wet weeds across the bottom of its searchcoil. If very noticeable changes occur in the sound, the searchcoil does not have effective shielding. Slight audio changes may be expected when wet grass passes over the top of a searchcoil.

Your searchcoil must be light, but it must also be sturdy and capable of rugged treatment. You want a tough exterior that will not abrade or tear easily on rough ground.

Searchcoils must withstand the greatest abuse of any detector component because they are constantly being slid across the ground, bumped into rocks and trees, submerged in water and generally mistreated in every way. Consequently, we manufacturers must exercise great care in construction. I urge you coin hunters to exercise similar care through the use of searchcoil covers, known sometimes as skid plates.

Garrett's new Crossfire searchcoil models feature a special innovation designed to permit them to take rugged treatment and keep providing top performance. This is a "tri-point" suspension that isolates the transmitter/receiver windings from shock and encapsulation stress. The winding arrays literally "float" within the searchcoil and do not respond to every bump and shock. The resulting stability permits winding the antennas for peak performance. The Crossfire coils also offer 100% scan width because of the effective method in which antennas are mounted. Effective pinpointing is guaranteed for targets at any depth.

All Garrett searchcoils have been subjected to rigorous testing in the laboratory and out in the fields and waters where hobbyists will expect them to perform. Field testing by the author of this book and other coin hunting experts has been a key ingredient in the successful performance of all Garrett equipment from the company's earliest days.

Never underestimate the importance of a searchcoil on your detector, and remember that searchcoils are manufactured in various sizes for specific reasons. Investigate and experiment! Learn which searchcoils operate best on your instrument for coin hunting as well as for other types of treasure hunting at which you may want to try your hand.

Finally, there is no such thing as a "standard searchcoil." The term *standard* is an absolute misnomer because the coil that operates ideally in a park may be next-to-useless on a junk-filled beach. The searchcoil that finds coins would rarely be used to search for a cache. Searchcoils come in a wide range of sizes.

Sizes

Let's review the various sizes and types of searchcoils that are available for the modern metal detector:

7-9″ Diameter: This size searchcoil is furnished with most detectors which is proper because such a searchcoil is usually the best size for coin hunting and other general purpose uses.

These searchcoils are lightweight, have good scanning width and are sensitive to a wide range of targets. Small objects can be detected, and good ground coverage can be obtained. Shallow scanning width is approximately equal to the diameter of the searchcoil. Depth of detection is satisfactory for most targets with a searchcoil of this size.

3-5″ Diameter: This size searchcoil is referred to as a Super Sniper by Garrett. Its intense electromagnetic field gives good detection of small objects, and its narrow pattern permits excellent target isolation and precise pinpointing. Depth of detection is not as great as that of larger sizes. Remember, however, that a searchcoil illuminates everything in the search matrix. In high junk areas it is possible to find coins with a Super Sniper that would be masked by junk signals if a larger coil were used.

12″ Diameter and Larger: Searchcoils of this size, while able to detect coins at great depths are also classified as the smallest searchcoils to be used for cache and relic hunting. Precise pinpointing is obviously more difficult with the larger sizes, and their increased weight usually necessitates the use of an armrest or hip-mounted control housing, especially when the detector is used for long periods.

Of course, you will want to use this larger searchcoil when searching deeply for coins or any other treasures. But, when you are hunting coins, how do you know when to switch from your "standard" size to the larger searchcoil? Suppose you locate a target in the fringe area of detection. You know from the

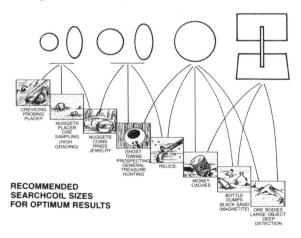

**RECOMMENDED
SEARCHCOIL SIZES
FOR OPTIMUM RESULTS**

weak audio signals that you are at the outer edges of your detector's capability with this searchcoil. By using a larger size, you will generally detect deeper.

Other Types: There are still other types of searchcoils such as the elliptical-shaped models and the Depth Multiplier, the so-called two-box unit that is used for ultra-deep detecting. Of course, the Depth Multiplier is definitely not suited to coin hunting nor should it ever be used when coins are a primary target. Garrett's "Bloodhound" Depth Multiplier is recommended in the search for money caches, large relics, safes, cannons, ore veins and mineral structures.

The elliptical coil is a different story.

Elliptical Coils: Initially designed for electronic prospecting where it could fit between rocks into places where a round coil could not search effectively, newly designed elliptical coils have proven to be amazingly successful coin-finders. Because of their electronic design and shape these coils have a "knife-edge" searching pattern that pierces deeply through tough minerals and trash. Thus, a 5x10-inch elliptical coil offers the effective searching width of a 10-inch circular coil but concentrates its detection pattern over a narrow area.

To improve your general education in all phases of treasure hunting I urge to learn about these other types of searchcoils and to practice using them whenever you have a chance.

Chapter 19

Detector Features

T he chapter after this one will review the basic types of detectors that are most commonly used today for finding coins. Now, however, I want to discuss four important features that are common to all detectors. A thorough understanding of each of these features is essential to your success as a coin hunter.

- **Ground Balance**
- **Discrimination**
- **Pinpointing**
- **Audio**

Of course, each of these four topics is vital in almost any aspect of metal detecting, as well as coin hunting. Because these topics are so important to the hobby, any time two or more coin hunters get together, you're liable to hear several different opinions about each of them. So, here are my thoughts on these important subjects:

Ground Balance

This metal detector feature still remains one of the most important for coin hunters—whether it be performed manually or automatically. Because the function is automatic on most detectors that are made today, many hobbyists never realize its absolute importance.

For many years ground balance was an area of considerable concern—and no small difficulty—to all users of metal detectors...if we could measure it by the volume of calls received at the factory. And, our dealers would tell us how their customers also appeared to have problems. I could easily understand why ground balance was such a concern, yet I have known for years that the day would come when ground balance would scarcely even be considered by most hobbyists—even those whose instruments offer manual ground balancing.

This is proving true today for operators of our new Grand Master Hunter CX II and III and Master Hunter CX metal detectors. These detectors provide *precise* ground balance automatically and instantly, no matter what type of terrain or material is below the searchcoil, and regardless of the mode of operation. Operators of this new equipment truly never need to worry about ground balance.

I completed my test phase with this detector circuitry over some of the most highly mineralized ground to be found anywhere; namely, in an area 12 miles west of Quartzsite, AZ, and another area near Scottsdale, AZ. Results were literally unbelievable!

Automatic Ground Balance

For the users of our GTA and Freedom models ground balance is never a problem because it is performed automatically...with control levels set at the factory. That is the case with most other detectors manufactured today. Now, any instruments with automatic ground balance should not be expected to achieve the extreme depth possible with a true All Metal non-motion mode, but the trade-off (depth for ease-of-operation) is one that has satisfied most hobbyists.

Yet, there can still no doubt that ground balance, whether performed automatically or manually, will always be one of the most important features of metal detector circuitry. Many veteran coin hunters would argue the importance of depth, and some might opt for discrimination. The simple fact remains, however, that without precise ground balance—performed either automatically or manually—coin hunting as we know it today would not be possible in most soil. Why not? Because most soils contain just too darned much mineralization.

You beginning coin hunters with a new detector may quickly grow accustomed to the excellent ground balance available on today's modern automatic detector; you may even take this feature for granted. *Please don't!* Some old-timers are still in awe at the ease with which today's modern detectors ground balance themselves. These veterans will assure you that ground balance is very important. And, as you progress in the hobby, you will soon agree. In fact, there will be many times when precise manual ground balance will be demanded if you are to achieve optimum results...especially if you want to hunt for deep caches or for gold.

If your detector offers manual ground balance, learn all you can about it. It will probably be as important as anything you ever do after you turn on the instrument and set the audio.

Why Ground Balance?

Just why is ground balancing so vital? Let's first understand exactly what is meant by the term. As discussed earlier, there are two predominant ground minerals that concern us. They are wetted salt and iron, and they can be found literally all over the world. Wetted salt can be found predominantly at ocean beaches but also at numerous upland locales. Iron minerals, generally classified further as non-conductive (not metal) minerals, can be found practically everywhere.

Both wetted salt and iron are readily detectable and cause untold grief to conventional detectors unless some means is available to cancel or "ground balance" them out. The term, ground balance, then is our description of the method of electronic circuitry that enables a metal detector to ignore these minerals completely...to go about its business of detecting other metals as if iron and wetted salt were not even present.

The motion mode of detecting has been around several years and is available on detectors from a number of manufacturers, including Garrett's GTA and Freedom models. It is also available on all of the CX-designated models. As its name implies, the motion mode requires that the detector be continually moving (in motion) to detect objects. This mode is very efficient and quite good for hunting coins. Both salt and iron minerals are essentially ignored by motion circuitry, permitting the hobbyist to concentrate on finding coins without being bothered by detection of minerals.

Motion vs. Non-Motion

Two basic detector modes of operation are motion and non-motion. The non-motion mode, permitting a detector's coil to hover perfectly still, gives the best performance for all types of treasure hunting. Detectors that employ the motion mode must always be in some slight motion to detect metal.

Non-motion ground balance was formerly achieved only through manual adjustment of controls. While such adjustments could be made with relative ease, it had been our desire (and, perhaps, that of other manufacturers) to produce detectors that were *fully automatic.*

The Grand Master Hunter CX II and CX III and the Master Hunter CX detectors, all with computerized circuitry based on microprocessor controls, offer motion as well as non-motion hunting modes. And, the motion mode features automatic ground balance and full discrimination control. Coin hunters have come to love the performance of these detectors.

Until today's computerized detectors were developed non-motion ground balancing was possible only through adjustment of manual controls. Whether such a task was complicated or not, only the operator could decide. I know that it was a chore that I never enjoyed.

The CX II and CX III are equipped with *Fast Track™* and *Ground Track™* automatic circuitry that balance out iron ground minerals automatically and continually, even as the searchcoil is being scanned. Such ground balancing occurs whether the searchcoil is moving or not. Even when the earth

Facing

Detectors should be capable of using different searchcoils such as the large 12 1/2-inch model on this Grand Master Hunter CX III.

Over

Note the built-in arm rest for ease of using this pistol-grip GTA detector that was designed primarily for hunting coins.

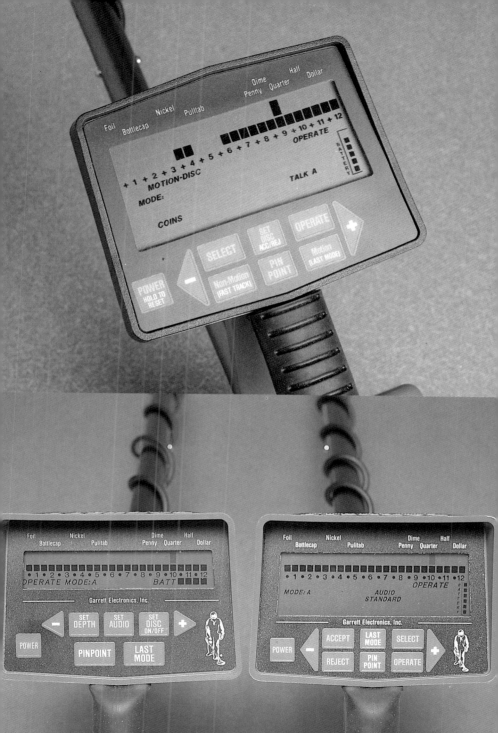

minerals themselves change density beneath the searchcoil, the Ground Track circuits sense these changes and properly adjust the detector's ground balancing characteristics...even as the detector is being scanned.

In its non-motion All Metal mode ground balancing on the Master Hunter CX is achieved *instantly* any time the Fast Track touchpad is pressed.

These new detectors, indeed, are *thinking* detectors, the detectors of tomorrow. But, today there remain in the hands of treasure hunters thousands of detectors that respond to manual ground balancing controls in the non-motion mode. The following "how to" discussion is concerned with such detectors and will be important to their operators.

Operators of Grand Master Hunters and Scorpion Gold Stingers who prefer to ground balance their instruments manually should also follow these instructions.

To Ground Balance Manually

First, you are urged to study the Owner's Manual for your particular detector. Read especially carefully the section concerning ground balance and relate it to the following instructions for manually ground balancing your own detector in the field.

Begin by holding the instrument with the searchcoil away from any metal and about two or three feet above the ground. Listen to the audio as you lower the searchcoil to operating height. If the audio signal grows or fades to any degree, you will require manual ground balancing.

Facing
A "secret of success" is how Charles Garrett describes personal testing of his detectors in direct comparison with competitive models.

Over
Note touchpads and Graphic Target Analyzers on control panels of Grand Master Hunter CX III, above, and GTA 1000, lower right, and GTA 500.

This procedure, of course, may differ from one brand to another. Basically, however, if the audio signal grows louder, turn down the ground balance control dial or press the button on your manual ground balance controls marked minus (-) several times. Lift your searchcoil again, press the audio (threshold) control and lower it again to operating height. If the sound level now decreases, you have made too great a negative adjustment. It will be necessary for you to press the touchpad marked plus (+) a few times or turn up your control dial. Remember that with the dial on a Garrett or other quality detector you are dealing with a 10-turn control for precise adjustment. Don't be afraid to turn it several times! Repeat these procedures until the audio does not change or changes only slightly when the searchcoil is lowered to operating height. When performing this ground balancing procedure, make certain there are no metal targets in the ground beneath your searchcoil.

When searching extremely mineralized ground, we recommend that you operate the searchcoil two inches or more above the ground. You will not lose depth, but will actually detect deeper because ground mineral influence is greatly reduced.

Discrimination

You can minimize digging and still not miss valuable targets by using discrimination properly.

It's sometimes difficult for those of us who have been hunting with metal detectors for a three decades or more to accept the ease and precise nature of modern discrimination circuits. We remember when any discrimination was considered "too much," and many veterans still urge you to dig all targets. Yet, I must admit that many of these same old-timers can be found dialing in "just a little" discrimination to permit them to miss some of the trash that always seems to be present in the soil.

As discussed earlier, Garrett's CX detectors and some other modern instruments feature two basic modes of operation—Discriminate (motion) and All Metal (non-motion).

In the Discriminate mode the operator can utilize discrimination controls to designate the type metal targets that are desired. In the All Metal mode, of course, *all* targets are audio- detected. But, remember this one very important point: In both modes the target ID meter continues to identify all detected targets. Here's a tip: operate in the motion All Metal mode to achieve the greatest possible depth, and simply read the meter to identify detected targets!

This is particularly applicable to our new Ultra GTA detectors with their revolutionary *Graphic Target Analyzer*™ as more and more coin hunters learn to use the unique notch discrimination controls of this detector to find coins that other instruments leave behind.

Several Garrett detectors, as well as those of other manufacturers, feature dual discrimination controls. They offer multiple selectivity and the ability to reject and accept targets in both the ferrous—iron, or course—and non-ferrous ranges. The two controls split the full range of discrimination between ferrous and non-ferrous. Detection of iron objects such as nails, some foil, iron bottlecaps and small pieces of junk is controlled by one knob. The other control governs discrimination of such non-ferrous items as aluminum pulltabs and aluminum screwtops.

Each of the two controls operates independently. The setting of one has no effect whatsoever on the other. If you wish to detect all ferrous materials, rotate the ferrous control of your detector to zero (fully counterclockwise on Garrett controls). As you advance it back to the right to higher numbers, you will reject more and more ferrous materials. The control operates cumulatively; that is, if you have it set at bottlecap rejection, most nails and some foil will be rejected along with bottlecaps. We urge that you advance this control no farther clockwise than necessary to eliminate the troublesome ferrous junk material in the ground you are searching.

Operate your non-ferrous control in the same manner. When it is turned fully to the left, few of the non-ferrous materials will be rejected. To eliminate, say, pulltabs, rotate the control clockwise to the manufacturer's suggested setting for them. Keep in mind, however, that there appear to be as many different kind of pulltabs as there are canning companies. Some few pulltabs, especially those that are bent or broken, seem to be acceptable to any detector at any setting. Set your controls for those you are finding just in the area where you are hunting.

Setting DISC Controls

Here's how to set any of those discrimination controls precisely: Collect examples of the types of junk you want to reject—a nail, bottlecap, pulltab and, perhaps, small pieces of iron trash. Place your detector on a non-metallic, preferably wooden, surface with the searchcoil at least three feet away from all metal. Make certain you are wearing no rings or jewelry on our hands or arms that could be detected. Rotate both control knobs (or only one, if your instrument is so designed) fully counterclockwise to the lowest settings. Turn the detector on and listen for the tone telling you it is ready to operate. Adjust the audio control for threshold sound.

If you have an Ultra GTA detector you can follow these instructions to learn more about discrimination notches. Set your GTA 1000 to its All Metal or your GTA 500 to Mode A. (Both should have ALL 24 Lower Scale segments displayed.)

Pass the iron bottlecap across the bottom of your searchcoil about two inches away from it. Your detector will probably make a signal. Rotate the ferrous control to the approximate bottlecap reject position or the setting suggested by your manufacturer, and pass the cap across the searchcoil's bottom again. You should hear nothing more than, perhaps, a slight blip. You may be able to rotate the control counterclockwise back to a lower number and still not detect the bottlecap. Practice so that you can set your control as far to the left as possible because you always want to use the lowest setting that is required.

Using the same technique, adjust the non-ferrous control just far enough clockwise that you do not detect the aluminum pulltab. This should be approximately the manufacturer's suggested setting point, which should probably prove to be your optimum pulltab setting, with the settings necessary for other style pulltabs being both above and below this one determined point. Again, let us stress that you should rotate these controls no higher than necessary to reject the junk items in the ground where you are searching.

With your GTA detector follow instructions to "turn off" the Lower Scale segment beneath the indicator of the target you want to discriminate against. This creates a discrimination notch.

Dual discrimination controls such as those on Garrett detectors offer a greater dynamic adjustment range than single controls. You have more resolution which allows you to set the controls precisely to reject specific junk targets. A most important feature is that you can reject most aluminum pulltabs while accepting the majority of gold and silver rings. When searching for rings in a pulltab-infested area such as a beach, set your non-ferrous control no farther clockwise than necessary to eliminate most of the pulltabs. Rings with a higher conductivity—and, especially, mass—than pulltabs will be accepted. Remember, however, that some rings will fall into the lower, or ferrous, range. Thus, dual discrimination lets you select rings that register both "above" and "below" pulltab rejection. So, don't advance either control any farther clockwise than absolutely necessary.

There is another important reason for setting your discrimination controls conservatively. When a modern detector locates a junk target that you have asked it to discriminates against, it cancels out this junk target with a negative audio response that you normally cannot even hear. As you know, however, good targets generate a positive response which you love to hear. If both positive and negative targets are beneath your searchcoil simultaneously, the two responses tend to cancel one another, and you may miss a good find. Of course, the situation is rarely that simple. Depth of targets, their metallic content, size and many other factors must be considered. So, simply remember this: never use more discrimination than you absolutely need.

Pinpointing

Electronic pinpointing can hasten your recovery of coins and make treasure hunting more pleasurable as well.

Most veteran treasure hunters pride themselves in their ability to pinpoint targets using only the detectors normal search modes. Modern instruments make pinpointing so much easier that we old timers should swallow our pride and take advantage of the electronic assistance available to us. I know that I do! Who knows? The time we save might let us recover that "big one" that's always just around the corner.

Of course, you should check the Owner's Manual of your detector for proper understanding and use of its pinpointing function. But, a button or trigger somewhere on the detector will usually activate pinpointing circuitry. After you have detected a target, move the searchcoil off to the side, press and hold the Pinpoint touchpad (or switch) and scan your target area again. You will notice that signals have probably grown sharper to aid you in locating your target more precisely.

Meters on some detectors will further aid in recovery by indicating target depth. Actual depth, however, often depends on the size coil being used. The meter on Garrett's CX II and CX detectors will indicate target depth of coin-sized targets, no matter what size of coil is on the detector. Garrett's new detectors offer even more pinpointing help. The Graphic Target Analyzer on the Ultra GTA's reports depth of coins in inches, and *TreasureTalk* on the CX III will *tell* you how many inches deep your coin is buried!

Here's a tip for the ultimate in target pinpointing. Once you have determined the surface location where you believe the target to be buried, place your searchcoil lightly on the ground above it and activate the pinpoint control. Continue holding this control and slide the searchcoil back and forth over the target at the same operating height. You will notice very slight blips when the target is directly beneath the center of your searchcoil. If you can't notice these blips, perhaps you have elevated the searchcoil from its level when you first selected the Pinpoint mode. Try the procedure again a few times. Maintain constant searchcoil height, and you'll be amazed at your precise electronic pinpointing ability. Warning: this technique requires practice...but practice pays off!

Here are two methods that might prove helpful if your instrument does not offer electronic pinpointing. After you locate your target, continue moving its coil over the spot while reducing your audio level down almost into the quiet zone. You'll soon find your target signal weakening to a soft audio "blip." Your coin will be directly beneath the center of your coil where the loudest signal over your detected metal object now occurs.

The second method is to begin raising your searchcoil higher in the air each time you pass over the detected target. Once again, signals will get weaker and weaker until you can hear only a "blip." Again, the target will be underneath the maximum signal area. This second method is obviously more difficult because the height of your coil will make it harder for you to locate the exact spot on the ground.

Rely on electronic pinpointing! That's my advice.

Audio

Because the audio setting is one of the most important adjustments you make in learning to hunt coins with a metal detector, we strongly urge your close attention to this subject. I believe that maximum detection capability can be achieved only by adjusting the audio volume until you hear just the faintest sound coming from your speaker or headphones. This is very important! This faintest sound that you can hear is the detector's most sensitive operating point. It is called your threshold, which you will find to be a common term in all metal detector literature. You will notice that when you set the threshold to a very faint sound and then plug in your headphones, the threshold may be too loud. Simply turn the audio control knobs lightly to reduce the sound level back to your faint threshold level.

For some reason certain hobbyists prefer to operate a detector with what is called a silent threshold; that is, with absolutely no sound coming from the speaker or headphones. Some manufacturers even *promote* this method as a feature of their instrument. Of course, there is nothing "exclusive" about a silent threshold since it can be achieved with any detector. Yet I would personally never hunt this way. If you are determined, however, to use this silent threshold, we urge that you reach it by setting your audio to a slight level of sound, then backing off just enough to achieve silence. This adjustment insures that any detection sound will go above the silent threshold you are maintaining. Be certain to check occasionally to make certain that you remain at this audio level just below sound.

For maximum success a coin hunter should use headphones whenever searching with a metal detector. They are essential in noisy areas, such as the beach and near traffic. They enhance audio perception by bringing the sound directly into one's ears while masking outside noise interference.

Most persons can hear weaker sounds and detect deeper coins when quality headphones are used. They come in several sizes and configurations, the most popular being stereo types that cover the ears. For those detectors without volume controls headphones can offer the control that allow a wide degree of loudness adjustment without degrading the sound quality.

You should know that reducing sound volume to silent on a detector is accompanied by loss of detection depth and sensitivity. I strongly recommend that detectors always be operated with the audio control adjusted so that just a faint sound (threshold) can be heard. Headphones allow this threshold to be set much lower than with a speaker, giving improved performance. As an added benefit, headphones use considerably less power than a detector's speaker which results in the economy of longer battery life. And, you don't have to take the trouble to change them as often, either!

Chapter 20

Coin Hunting
Detectors

This chapter will discuss the three types of VLF (very low frequency) metal detectors now in greatest use as coin hunting instruments. And, it is definitely one of these three types that I would recommend for anyone who seeks to pursue this hobby or to become more proficient in it:

—**Automated**
—**Manual Adjust**
—**Computerized**

Some of you old-timers may immediately cry out that I've omitted your favorite detector, that wonderful old BFO or TR instrument that's found so many coins for you. Well, I'll just say two things about those old detectors and not mention them again:

1. They're obsolete. Newcomers to the hobby have no business using them. (And neither do old-timers, either! I wonder just how many coins those "wonderful" old detectors have actually scanned right over?)

2. You must already know more about them than I do because I certainly wouldn't try to use one to hunt coins . . . or anything else!

You may also notice that I will not discuss the pulse induction detectors that were included in my first coin hunting book. Let me add, quickly, that pulse detectors are highly capable instruments that I rate very highly for coin hunting, especially on the beach, in the surf or in the ocean's depths. The fact is, however, that the only pulse detectors now being commercially manufactured are submersible models for hunting under water. Our Sea Hunter is protected to depths of 200 feet. Since this a feature not especially desired by most coin hunters, this type of instrument will not be discussed here. If you're interested in the pulse detector or underwater hunting generally, I recommend my *Treasure Recovery from Sand and Sea.*

Automated (Motion)

The motion-type VLF detector with automatic ground balance is probably the most popular model generally used today for hunting coins. First of all, it is easy to use. Added to this are its capabilities for finding coins and jewelry that are almost equal to those of the higher priced detectors. This capability becomes particularly apparent when both expensive and average-priced models are in the hands of a novice.

Of course, various models of the automated detectors are manufactured today. Some offer more features than others, and some are simply better than others. Working with a dealer and trying out various detectors will enable you to determine which model is best suited for your needs.

Automated VLF instruments are often referred to as "motion" detectors since they can be hovered over a target for only a few seconds because of their automatic circuitry. Consequently, slight searchcoil motion is always necessary. Certain models, however, can be scanned much more slowly than others. You must learn the capabilities of your instrument through practice.

Another technique you will have to practice is pinpointing, especially on manicured lawns where exact location is important. Since hovering over a target is not possible, manual pinpointing will be more difficult for some operators than for others. Electronic pinpointing found on all the better models adequately overcomes this deficiency. Simply stated, however, pinpointing generally presents no problem with any coin hunting detector because coins must be considered comparatively large targets.

The automated VLF instrument ranks high among all types of detectors in detection depth. Not only is it capable of reaching to great depths to detect coins, but its extremely sharp, fast response signal is unmistakable when coins and other objects are detected.

It would be well to warn against confusing automatic ground

balance with the "automatic tuning" feature on some models of older detectors. This feature is concerned only with the audio

The Garrett Museum contains a complete exhibit of the most modern treasure hunting equipment. Bob Podhrasky, chief Company engineer, holds a new computerized detector.

threshold of the detector and has no relationship to ground balance.

All quality automated VLF detectors will offer some form of trash elimination through discrimination control(s). I urge you to read the section on this feature in the preceding chapter to insure that you realize the full benefits offered by your detector.

I should point out here that many hobbyists find the automated VLF models fairly satisfactory for types of metal detecting other than coin hunting. This is particularly true of those produced by quality manufacturers. In fact, I've used our automated Freedom and Beach Hunter models for shallow relic hunting. Some hobbyists even report they have found gold nuggets with an automated instrument. If you're interested in a detector that will perform satisfactorily in situations other than coin hunting, however, I suggest that you read on about the manual adjust and computerized models.

Manual Adjust (Non-Motion)

Until the development of the automated VLF the manual adjust models dominated the coin hunting field. They represented such an improvement over the old BFO and TR detectors which had but limited (perhaps, non-existant would be a better description) ability to eliminate iron earth minerals and wetted salt. Quality manual adjust VLF's are still highly popular instruments capable of performing all coin hunting, treasure hunting and prospecting tasks. They detect very deeply and are offered to coin hunters with an array of desirable features.

Some modern computerized VLF detectors, such as the Grand Master Hunter, already include the automatic ground balancing feature. As I pointed out in the previous chapter of this book, I believe that in just a few years all quality VLF detectors will provide automatic ground balance. In fact, it will be a an aspect of metal detecting that hobbyists can take for granted! What an improvement this truly is . . . especially after all the problems that veteran THers have experienced over the years with ground balance.

Today, however, a large number of quality detectors already in the hands of treasure hunters permit the coin hunter to adjust ground balance manually. All of these instruments will fulfill every expectation of most coin hunters. In addition, the detectors can meet the requirements of cache hunters, relic hunters and electronic prospectors with ease and efficiency. Since quality VLF detectors are so highly capable, they can be selected and used with the utmost confidence.

I especially commend this type of detector to the individual who is interested in coin hunting but already has an "itch" to try out the other types of metal detecting. As noted above, many hobbyists use motion-type automated VLF detectors for tasks other than coin hunting. The simple fact of the matter is, however, that manual adjust non-motion models will generally function better than an automated detector in areas other than coin hunting.

Because of those selfsame "manual" controls from which it gets its name, this type of detector is capable of more precise ground balance. Such precision will rarely be required by the average coin hunter. Not so with relic and cache hunters who seek deep targets and electronic prospectors working over highly mineralized ground. They demand absolute ground balance that will enable them to hear faint signals from faraway or tiny targets.

Any kind of pinpointing technique is possible with the manual adjust VLF detectors since they can be hovered over a target at will. Still, the matter or pinpointing is not especially important since modern, quality instruments all offer precise electronic pinpointing circuitry.

The fact of the matter is that manual adjust VLF detectors are just a little more difficult to use than the automated VLF models because they have to be ground balanced. At the same time, however, they offer more versatility and will usually provide greater satisfaction in areas of metal detecting other than coin hunting. A manual adjust detector, therefore, can prove to be a valuable addition to your metal detecting equipment.

Computerized

The finest metal detectors available today – and, in the forseeable future – are instruments with computerized circuitry based on microprocessor controls such as the Grand Master Hunter.

Simply stated, the computerized detector is a *thinking*

machine; it performs literally millions of analytical computations almost simultaneously to make circuitry adjustments that were formerly made by hand by the hobbyist. As the searchcoil receives data, it is fed into microprocessor circuitry in digital form and compared with the "mind" of the computer, data that has been stored in the computer at the factory. Thus, knowledge that formerly was required from the operator is now in the computer which permits it to make adjustments that once required manual action. Not only does the computerized detector make these adjustments automatically, but they are made instantaneously—when they are needed, not when the need for them is finally noticed by an operator.

As the detector is scanned, it continually performs self-tests; that is, it self-adjusts to achieve optimum operating performance for all conditions, including battery condition, temperature changes, ground mineral variations and even the possible aging of electronic components that might cause "values" to change. Target data coming through the detector's searchcoil is compared with the particular requirements dialed in by the operator (such as discrimination) to produce the proper audio and meter indications. False signals, caused by conventional detector "back reading" are eliminated. Even large, surface and shallow objects are properly read on the meter with the precise audio tone given.

Garrett engineers have known for years that different ground mineral conditions cause different discriminating performance. Garrett's Grand Master Hunter CX III has various scanning methods stored in its memory bank. As earth mineralization changes while this detector is being scanned. the CX III automatically readjusts itself to use the optimum discrimination method.

Computerized detectors such as the Garrett Ultra GTA 1000 and 500, the Grand Master Hunter CX III and CX II or the Master Hunter CX permit the ultimate in coin hunting. No better instruments have ever been devised for the hobby. Greater depths and considerably more discriminating accuracy is possible. Additionally, these computerized detectors automatically monitor every external atmospheric and ground condition to maintain their circuitry at optimum levels. Of course, just as some of these capabilities that can be achieved with the computerized microprocessor-controlled detectors are not possible with conventional instruments, the capabilities may not be required by all coin hunters.

Yet Garrett's computerized instruments truly represent the finest coin hunting detectors ever developed. Modern circuitry and a genuine non-motion All Metal mode earn for the Grand Master Hunter CX III its coveted distinction as the *deepest seeking detector known to man*. Notch discrimination available on the CX III, as well as the GTA detectors, is ideally suited to coin hunting. In fact, Garrett engineers who developed the GTA instruments obviously had coin hunting in mind as the primary use of these detectors!

It has been said that operator "mistakes" can be virtually eliminated with the "thinking" detectors. I know that treasures are already being discovered that could never have been found before. I have seen them!

"Worked-out" areas are producing vast amounts of new coins. Because these new coins are ones that were buried more deeply or were masked by trash, they are usually older and more valuable than coins that had previously been found in the same areas.

Computerized detectors permit professional performance and detection accuracy to be achieved easily by beginners at levels that have tantalized professionals for years. We have truly entered the era of hi-tech metal detector performance. Coin hunting and all other forms of metal detecting will never be the same again.

Facing

Because valuables are believed to have been
hidden in the walls when this structure was built,
a Pocket Probe is being used to examine it.

Over

The Bloodhound Deepseeker coil extends a
detector's normal depth range two to four
times to search for caches and ore deposits.

Chapter 21

Detector Care

Modern metal detectors are precision electronic instruments that have been specially designed with many new components that can help direct coin hunters to valuable targets while helping them avoid specific items of metallic "trash."

Of course, the preceding paragraph along with all the other material in this book pertain only to *quality* metal detectors, such as those designed and produced by Garrett Electronics and other respected manufacturers. Quality must be engineered into a detector . . . then built into it at the factory. No amount of expertise in the technique of its operator can transform a poorly designed detector into a quality instrument for finding coins!

Any quality detector is built to withstand rugged treatment in the field. It is a piece of outdoor equipment, designed to help you

Facing
Above
This cache of silver coins hidden in a water pail and recovered with a metal detector at an old farm house is typical of those being found every day.
Below
Look at these beautiful coins! All of them were discovered by hobbyists using Garrett metal detectors and then displayed at the Company's museum.

Over

Beautiful collections of treasures such as this are the pride and joy of hobbyists who find these valuable objects in addition to the coins they seek.

find coins anywhere and under almost any conditions. You should always remember, however, that your detector is a precise electronic instrument and handle it with as much care as possible at all times. By all means, use it to the fullest, but only as it was intended. Treat it as you would any piece of electronic equipment and always protect it from mist, rain or blowing sand. Take time to clean it after each coin hunting expedition and try to keep it as clean as possible, especially when not in use.

If you will spend just a minimum amount of time caring for your detector on a timely basis, you can *avoid* many of the problems you may hear about from some hobbyists. Still, it's a fact of life that problems or difficulties sometimes occur to everyone. While suggesting what you can do to avoid them, this chapter will also discuss how you can deal most effectively with some of these situations.

If you give your instrument the reasonable care described in this chapter, it should easily provide more than five (actually, up to ten) years of uninterrupted service, barring some catastrophic failure of transistors or other components. And, I'm talking about perfect performance on a regular basis when you use your detector at least weekly, if not more often.

The first rule is to read your Owner's Manual thoroughly. We have discussed this subject elsewhere in this book, but I can't stress its importance strongly enough. You won't be able to care for your detector properly if you don't understand it. And, the first step to understanding an instrument is to learn all that the manufacturer and his dealer can tell you about the one they have designed, produced and sold to you.

Caring for your detector is not a complicated matter. In fact, the only things that you should really have to do are keep it clean and keep it supplied with fresh batteries. The subject of batteries is one that continually confronts every detector owner. It is important that you understand thoroughly how dry cell batteries relate to your metal detector.

Batteries

Batteries are the major source of detector problems!

There is no way that I can overemphasize the above statement. Our technicians at the Garrett factory are continually amazed at the number of detectors sent to us for repair when all they need is a new set of batteries!

So, whenever you find your detector inoperable . . . whenever it will not respond properly . . . whenever it is just plain "broke" . . . *check your batteries.* Without a doubt, weak or worn-out batteries or batteries that have jarred loose are the single, major cause of detector break-down. I don't intend to suggest that new batteries will always cure your detector's problems, but batteries many times are at least one source of the problem whenever a detector stops working. Always carry a fresh set of batteries with you whenever you are hunting. Even though your detector's meter or tone indicator reports that your batteries are satisfactory, test the detector with fresh batteries any time it fails.

Whenever you change batteries, make certain the new ones are inserted properly and test satisfactorily. Regularly check your detector's battery and power system. Inspect terminals for corrosion and tightness. Look for wires that might have been pinched when they were pulled out earlier while batteries were being changed. These pinched wires can set up a problem that leads to failure later in the field. If your detector's rechargeable battery compartment (or any part of the instrument, for that matter) is sealed at the factory, never try to open it. You may ruin your detector; at best, you'll void your warranty.

Four types of batteries are in general use in modern electronic metal detectors:

Carbon zinc batteries cost the least and deliver current for the shortest period of service. They operate most efficiently at temperatures (fahrenheit) from about 32 (freezing) to just over 100 degrees. They are more prone to leak than any other type of battery.

Heavy duty (zinc chloride) batteries are generally more expensive than carbon zinc, but will give longer service. They are more prone to leak than alkaline or NiCad batteries.

Alkaline (alkaline manganese) batteries cost more than carbon zinc and heavy duty types, but they generally provide current for considerably more hours. Furthermore, they last longer in storage, are less susceptible to leakage and perform better in extreme temperatures. Their use is probably cheaper in the long run than carbon zinc or heavy duty types.

NiCad (nickel cadmium) rechargeable batteries are more expensive than the other types because they are designed to be recharged easily (some manufacturers claim that they can be recharged one thousand times). Maximum life and best performance can be achieved if they are used often and recharged immediately at room temperature. Always remember that NiCad batteries will generally "take a set" if repeatedly used the same length of time. For example, if you consistently use your NiCad batteries for just one hour before recharging them, they will "take a set" of one hour, and that is the maximum length of time they will ever deliver current. For this reason you should occasionally let your NiCad batteries run down completely before recharging. In fact, you will extend the life of NiCad batteries if you will completely discharge them and restore a full charge at least once every three months.

NiCad batteries will generally power a circuit only 40 to 50% as long as carbon zinc batteries. For example, if your detector will operate for 20 hours on carbon zinc batteries, NiCads will power it from eight to ten hours. Since NiCad operating voltage is less than that of the other types, they register at a lower level on meters and lights designed to check batteries on detectors.

Tips on Care

Unless you take care of your detector you can't benefit fully from all the quality built into it. Quality detectors are truly "macho" machines. But, don't overdo it! Never forget that your detector is an electronic instrument. True, it is designed and manufactured to withstand rugged outdoor use, but you should always handle it as carefully as possible.

Try to avoid temperature extremes as much as possible, such as storing the detector in an automobile trunk during hot summer months or outdoors in sub-freezing weather.

For periods of storage longer than approximately one month, remove the batteries from the detector. Some coin hunters always remove batteries whenever their detector is not in use.

Before submerging *any part* of your detector in water for *any reason,* make certain that it is designed NOT to be damaged by water. Talk to your dealer; call the manufacturer, if necessary.

All Garrett searchcoils (and most of those of other quality manufacturers) are submersible to the cable connector. Unless specifically noted, however, the control housing of *no detector* is submersible. Therefore control housings must always be protected from mist, rain or blowing surf.

Oh, that's not to say that a drop or two (or, even three) of water or salt spray will damage a Garrett detector or one built by any of the other reputable manufacturers. All of them are made tough. But, once again – don't overdo it! Remember that fresh water will *probably* ruin the electronic components of any detector and salt water *certainly will!* Protect your control housing from water at all times.

Never place a metal detector or searchcoil in a heated oven for drying. Normal temperature is sufficient.

Keep your detector clean. Always wipe the housing after use and wash the coil when necessary. Protect your instrument from dust and sand as much as possible.

There will be times, especially after beach hunting, when your detector needs *special cleaning*. When it gets this dirty, you can follow these instructions:

Completely disassemble the detector stem and flush it with fresh water. A soapy solution can be used to aid removal of stubborn materials. Lubricants are not recommended under any circumstances unless they are positively non-sticky and will not attract dust particles or grit.

The searchcoil can be cleaned with a garden hose. Never let water get into the cable connector. Protect the cable from sharp blows at all times and be careful to avoid kinking it.

Wipe the control housing with a damp cloth. Open any portals and battery doors and check the interior. Clean out foreign material such as sand or leaves. Never use forced air to clean a detector. Air that is blown into a detector control housing can force dust and other debris to become lodged in electrical controls and cause them to fail.

Never use spray cleaners or lubricants on the printed circuit board or controls. Such materials leave harmful residues. Never use any petroleum products on or in your detector.

When using your detector, inspect all exposed connectors daily. Each time you change the batteries, inspect all battery and clip connections. Any contamination and corrosion can usually be removed with a pencil eraser. Be careful, however, not to short the terminals of the battery with the metal casing of the eraser. Any spring clips that appear to have been forced open should be closed, using only the pressure of your fingers. Visually inspect all detector components during maintenance and cleaning operations.

Field Maintenance

Most detector *failures* can be attributed to batteries that refuse to work or operators who refuse to think.

You may be surprised at how many areas there are in which you can determine the reason for your detector's problem. You can even remedy some of these problems; for others, you can devise "field expedients" that will let you keep on hunting temporarily. Of course, if any of these problems continues to occur, you should contact your dealer or the manufacturer immediately.

Basic Battery Tips — Make sure you insert new batteries correctly and that they test satisfactorily. Regularly give your detector a thorough visual examination. Check battery terminals for tightness. Carefully examine the detector by looking through any doors and portals and observe every component for damage. Look for pinched wires. When panels are replaced in changing batteries, wires can be pinched. Often, there is no immediate problem, but the potential exists for a failure in the field.

Searchcoil/Speaker Contamination—Foreign items such as dirt, black magnetic sand, small metal particles or other matter can work into a searchcoil cover or speaker to cause erratic sounds. These sounds are annoying and may cause you to think your detector's circuitry is faulty. You can easily clean your searchcoil cover. If magnetic particles are sticking to the speaker cone, hold the detector in such a position to let the particles fall out. Test your detector by activating it. Sometimes, the vibration of the speaker cone will loosen particles that have become magnetically attached to it. A small magnet can also be used to pull out sticky particles.

Cable Connector Inspection — Erratic sounds can result when your cable is slightly twisted at the point where it enters the cable connector clamp. To check for this problem remove the connector cable clamp screws, remove the clamp and visually inspect the wiring. Rotate the wire slightly to test for broken connections. If you have some knowledge of electronics or soldering, you can repair these immediately with a soldering iron. As soon as possible, however, let a reputable technician check your emergency repairs. Incidentally, some detector connectors are factory molded, which virtually eliminates broken connections.

Testing Searchcoils/Cables — Erratic operations or no audio can be the fault of the searchcoil and/or the cable. With your detector turned on gently twist the searchcoil back and forth. Pay close attention to the connection of the cable's point of entry into the searchcoil. Gently tug the cable to determine if wiring is broken. If wires break in the field, you can sometimes tape the searchcoil cable to bring the loose wires together so that you can finish that day's searching. Permanent repairs will be necessary, however, and I urge you to have them made as soon as possible. Never expect a field expedient to provide a *permanent* solution to your problem. Generally, a broken cable cannot be repaired; the searchcoil must be replaced.

Intermittent Sounds — Check your battery connections, even if you have been inspecting them regularly. Check closely for corroded batteries. Sometimes batteries will leak a small amount of acid, creating corrosion on the contacts.

Non-detection — If your detector will not detect metal — even a coin lying on top of the ground — make certain that its circuitry is properly ground balanced. Also, check to see if you have turned your discrimination control(s) too high.

Audio Threshold Drift — If your audio threshold won't hold but drifts up and down, check your batteries. In addition, some detectors will require warm-up time. Make sure you have allowed adequate time (five minutes or so) for the detector's circuitry to warm up. When you take a detector from an air conditioned car and operate it in hot sunlight, components can heat too rapidly, necessitating a few minutes warmup time.

Detector "Quits" When Searchcoil Is Submerged — Even searchcoils that are guaranteed submersible to the cable connector have been known to leak. Sometimes the cable or searchcoil covering has been punctured by careless handling or by thorns or other sharp pointed objects. Searchcoils can be punctured under water by coral. Water then seeps into the searchcoil, causing the searchcoil to fail temporarily. Searchcoils have been known to leak when taken from a hot car and immediately submerged in extremely cold water. When hot air in the searchcoil is cooled quickly by the water, a vacuum forms and pulls in water through even the tiniest crack in the cable or searchcoil.

If you suspect water seepage in your searchcoil, let it dry for a few days in a warm place (not an oven!). If you can locate where the water has seeped into the cable or coil, you can make permanent repairs with liquid silicone. Apply it generously to the puncture and let dry thoroughly before using. Searchcoil covers (or, skidplates) are recommended because they will protect your coil against accidental punctures.

Water in Detector Housing — This is awful! At best you will have to return your instrument to the factory for thorough inspection and overhaul. At worst . . . you can imagine. Even if you carefully protect your detector while surf hunting or searching in the rain, there's a way water can still get into some housings. If you've been in or around water, never elevate the searchcoil above the level of the control housing because any water in the stem may flow right back into your housing. Always check the stem for accumulated water and carefully drain it.

Intermittent Audio/Unsteady Threshold — You'll probably find this caused by operating too near high voltage power lines, radio/TV transmission facilities or lines, airports or another metal detector. Even CB radios can cause you a problem! Try changing your detector's frequency, if it has this capability. Otherwise, move to another location.

You might also unplug your headphone to see what sound your detector's speaker provides. Perhaps the wires to your headphones have been damaged. If so, you can try to continue searching with only the speaker.

Short Battery Life — If this happens with NiCads, read the

Battery section of this chapter and note the comments about a "set." If normal batteries are being used, change to new ones that you know are absolutely fresh and keep careful records on their useful life. Headphones require far less power than your detector's speaker. When you use them, your detection efficiency will increase as well.

No Detection Depth—If your batteries are strong; if your detector is correctly ground balanced; if you have good audio, the problem probably lies not with your detector . . . but, with you. Of course, searchcoils have been known to fail. Try using a different one. If you still can't get very much depth, go back to your Owner's Manual. Read it again and follow its instructions carefully.

When It Must Return to the Factory—Pack the detector and defective searchcoil(s) carefully with lots of insulation. Do not return stems or headphones unless you suspect they are part of the problem. Always return at least one of your searchcoils (the one you use the most) even when you are convinced they operate satisfactorily. Of course, always return the battery tray, if your detector is so equipped. Do not pack digging tools, which only increase weight. By all means enclose a letter with your name, address and a complete but concise description of your problem; i.e., how often it occurs and the special conditions that seem to cause it.

You would be amazed at the small number of Garrett detectors that are *ever* returned to the factory for repairs or for any other reason. Quality detectors are well-made instruments that perform the tasks for which they are designed. Use them to carry out these tasks, and you and your detector will have a long and happy life together. You can take my word for it!

Chapter 22
Still More Tips

I t's difficult for me to understand why people would spend their hard-earned money for a modern detector and then refuse to learn to use it correctly. You must learn all about your instrument and practice with it to achieve the best results. Read the Owner's Manual for your detector not once but several times. Follow this by *using* your instrument. In our Garrett Owner's Manuals we recommend that you build your own test plot. Bury several items, including a nail, a piece of foil, a pull-tab, a bottlecap and several coins at depths of about two to eight inches and a foot apart. Clearly mark the location where each article is buried. Practice scanning the targets while listening to and studying the detection signals.

Try to understand fully that there is a lot to learn about your detector. Read *this* book thoroughly along with several other books on metal detection. A list of the Ram books accompanied by an order blank is at the back of this volume. Of course, if you're still reluctant to make the effort, here's the "easy" way to find coins. Follow the advice given by "Pinky" Nobel . . . cut a hole in your pocket, put some coins in this pocket and follow yourself around. As long as you keep putting coins in your pocket, you'll find plenty of them on the ground!

Scanning

To scan with your detector it is best to let the searchcoil overlap with each sweep. In other words, after you make each sweep with an 8 1/2-inch searchcoil, move ahead approximately four to five inches for the next sweep. This will give you the overlapping to insure that you are completely covering a given area.

I'm often asked how rapidly a hobbyist should scan in the search for coins. It's a mistake to scan too slowly just as it is to scan too rapidly. The novice should begin by scanning at the rate of about one foot per second. After several hours of practice (and, success in interpreting signals to find coins), scanning speed can be gradually increased. I recommend that you not attempt to scan faster than about two feet per second. At speeds faster than this only the most veteran coin hunters can be successful. At the same time, however, I urge you to work toward increasing your scanning speed. You'll be able to cover large areas more quickly and greatly increase your take.

Swinging a Coil

Most detector operators – beginners, I'm certain – swing their searchcoil in front of them in an arc. More experienced coin hunters move their coils in front of them in a straight line. I prefer the straight line method because I consider it far superior to swinging a coil in a arc. When you scan using straight lines, a much wider path can be covered in a single scan; the coil can be held at a more even height throughout the full scan; the hobbyist can cover an area more efficiently without skipping spots. Moreover, the straight line method gives the best exercise.

If you haven't tried scanning a straight line with your searchcoil, see for yourself how much better it is. You may find it awkward at first, but you'll soon get the "swing" of it!

Swing the searchcoil from side to side in front of you in a straight line. If you make sweeps wider than approximately four feet, it will be necessary at the end of each sweep for you to twist slightly or rotate your body at the hips (good exercise). Your feet will have to be approximately 18 inches to two feet apart to make the extra wide sweeps. As you approach the end of each sweep, you will see how easy it is to keep your searchcoil at the same height above the ground throughout the sweep. If you practice this method and work up a good rhythm, I believe you will actually enjoy this exercise . . . especially when you find coins with it!

Cover the Area

If you are confronted with a large area, and you are not sure if that area will be productive for coins, it is best to criss-cross it with a few well-planned passes. One method is to make a complete pass across one side of the area. Then, move over ten feet or so and make a second pass parallel to the first. Make notes when you find coins . . . exact location, depth, etc. Never make an attempt to begin scanning in any large area until you have done all you can to determine where the "hot spots" are.

Experienced coin hunters utilize several techniques to make certain thay have completely searched a large area. Sometimes they block it off into smaller areas, either mentally or by using some sort of markers. The smaller areas are then searched, one at a time, until the entire large area has been covered. In places where there are trees, benches and other natural markers, it is easy for the operator to cover the ground completely without any skipping. In open areas such as large fields and parks, you'll have to furnish your own markers.

Some hobbyists drive small stakes (or, golf tees) into the ground and tie strings between the stakes. They make their first pass along the length of the string with the side of the searchcoil touching it. At the end of the length of strip, they move the string over the width of a searchcoil scan and repeat the pro-

Charles Garrett demonstrates the straight-line, side-to-side method of scanning with a searchcoil which permits it to cover more ground with the coil kept at a constant height.

cess. Some people utilize only the sticks in the ground and leave off the string . . . which is satisfactory for a short distance. The more experienced you become, the easier it will be for you to search large areas. You will rely less and less on such markers as sticks and strings.

But, cover the entire area you intend to search. You must! Don't be in a hurry. The coin you are looking for and hurrying to find on the other side of the park may be right at your feet. Take your time and do a thorough job.

Super Sniping

Many coin hunters have realized they can find even more coins with *smaller* coils. I'm talking about Garrett's famed "Super Sniper" 4 1/2-inch Crossfire searchcoil. This small coil can search tight, narrow locations that won't accept larger searchcoils. In addition, it works especially well in trashy areas because the coil's small size lets it cover only a small area that can't include too many junk targets. Remember that a searchcoil reports on *all* targets in the search matrix that lies beneath it. When there are a lot of trash items, good coins can be masked.

When the Super Sniper coil was first made, our engineers envisioned it as a coil to find tiny gold nuggets . . . which it has! Coin hunters quickly learned about the new, smaller coil and have since used it to a far greater extent even than the electronic prospectors for whom it was intended. One East Coast hunter found more than 100 coins along and around the foundations of a destroyed apartment complex. "The coil's small size, its powerful, highly concentrated signal and its totally negative backreading were the main factors in making these finds," he said.

Coin hunters using the Super Sniper have learned to work more slowly and methodically and to expect a little shallower detection depth. One of these small coin hunting wonders makes a welcome addition to any coin hunter's arsenal of metal detecting accessories because it will make discoveries that larger searchcoils often miss.

Working Near Metal

Because of its small size, the Super Sniper lets a coin hunter work closer to such metal items as fences, playground equipment, parking meters and sign posts and buildings with metal siding. When a hobbyist is hunting with an 8 1/2-inch or larger coil, the metal in these objects prevents the operator from scanning up close, unless that operator knows how to deal with this situation. Here's what I recommend.

Search with your detector as you normally would until it begins to respond to the nearby metal object. When this occurs, adjust your audio volume down almost into the quiet zone and scan parallel to the object. Scan in a wide circle around posts. Then, listen closely for the increase in sound that will indicate a target. Since few treasure hunters have mastered this technique or know anything about it, you might find yourself with a real bonanza in some of your regular hunting spots.

Remember, however, the Super Sniper searchcoil offers the most effective method for scanning close to metal objects.

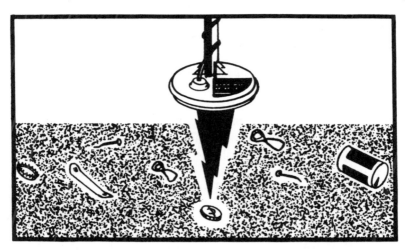

Because a "Super Sniper" searchcoil is smaller, it illuminates fewer targets, enabling the hobbyist to locate valuable coins that would be masked by signals from trash or hidden.

False Signals

Earlier in the book, I made the statement that your detector will never lie to you. I stand by that statement!

Still, I get complaints about "false" signals. Years ago, I remember talking to a man who said he got a faint signal near the trunk of a tree. He dug down a few inches and could find nothing. His detector produced the same signal. He dug into the tree roots and still found nothing. Yet, his detector still signaled a target! Finally, he found himself digging beneath the tree roots with nothing to show for his efforts but the faint signal. That's when he called me. "What do I do?" he asked.

"Get out of the hole and try somewhere else!" I told him. This is a good example of a person who did not know what to expect of his instrument and had not learned to use it correctly.

Occasionally I hear about a person thinking he has dug a false hole when he gets a signal, cuts a plug and then can get no signal either from the plug or the hole itself. Here's what may have happened. The coin might have become dislodged from the plug during your digging and fallen into the loose dirt at the bottom of the hole where it is standing in a vertical position. Because it is no longer lying flat in the ground, you can't get a signal from it. So, even though your detector no longer gives a signal from that hole, dig out a little more and sift the dirt through your fingers.

Foil can also create the impression of a false hole after it produces a metallic response on your detector. When you are digging, the small piece of foil crumples or becomes rolled up into a tiny ball. Then, there's no signal, either from the dirt you dug up or from the hole itself. Foil explains the mystery.

Repeat: your detector will never lie to you. But, it sometimes takes practice to understand what it is saying!

What a successful treasure hunt it was...and all hunts are a success if nobody gets hurt or spends money he or she can't afford!

Probes & Contouring

There are other methods that can be used to determine if you have metallic objects or a "false hole" under your searchcoil. You can use a probe rod two or three feet long of approximately 1/4 to 3/8-inch diameter. Rifle cleaning rods are good for this purpose, or you can devise your own rod as described elsewhere in this book. I know some treasure and cache hunters who will not dig any hole unless they probe. Some of my friends have become very adept with a probe. They can tell whether they've struck a rock, tin can, glass, wood or even when they encounter different types of soil. Some can even tell when their probe passes through an old newspaper, and I know of one man who claims to be able to *read* the newspaper . . . well, the headlines, at least!

Truthfully, however, whenever a probe touches a buried object it produces a reaction or vibration peculiar to the type of object. The vibrations are transmitted up the probe and into the hands of the operator.

Another method for determining if you have a false hole can be used where there is no problem in digging a large hole. What you have to do is to scoop out the ground in a bowl-shaped manner, the diameter of which is at least three times the diameter of your smallest coil. Then, scan the hole with your small coil, carefully following the contours. In that way the searchcoil will remain an equal distance from the ground whether it be the side or bottom of the hole. If it's only ground conditions that create your detector's signal, you'll get the same indications all over the hole. A pocket scanner really helps here. See Chapter 18 for a description.

Practice . . . practice . . . practice. Learn how to determine a "false hole" before you wear yourself out digging!

You may not find many coins in locales like this, but seeking all types of treasure with a metal detector will take you to such exciting places.

Chapter 23

Final Thoughts

To say that rewriting this grand old book was a labor of love would be a gross understatement. I can only hope that you have enjoyed reading it as much as I enjoyed writing it. There's so much to be said for the wonderful hobby of coin hunting with a metal detector that I could truly write another volume as large as this one.

In reviewing this work, however, I am convinced that enough completely new material is included here – along with all that was so popular with the old book – for any of you to improve your skills and for you novices to become proficient coin hunters . . . especially when you use a modern metal detector.

And, I sincerely hope that you will use a fine, new, modern detector. It will enhance your enjoyment of coin hunting so much, and will enable you truly to prove that the hobby will *pay for itself.*

This last statement was directed not only to beginners in the hobby but to you old-timers who are still using that obsolete "old favorite" of yours. You'll be amazed at the new models we can now offer you. Try one . . . I know you'll like it!

To close this book I'd like to review a couple of topics just a little more . . . to tell you how the hobby can pay for itself . . . to suggest that you join with others in the hobby and, finally to explain how you *will* want to expand your metal detecting interests beyond coin hunting. Plus, I'll offer some suggestions about how you can do these things.

Treasure Hunting

There is one fact that most coin hunters learn very quickly . . . the pursuit of wealth with a metal detector does not stop with coins! Perhaps they first discover this by digging up a valuable ring or gold chain. Then, they hear about a cache or have the opportunity to hunt in gold country . . . and, they're hooked for good!

Since complete research is a prime requisite in locating good places to coin hunt, you may soon find yourself somewhat of an amateur historian. As you pursue your research, don't overlook all the other things of value that can be found by using a metal detector. All forms of treasure hunting should be seriously considered as you go about your coin hunting. Other major areas of interest in treasure hunting are cache hunting, relic hunting and electronic prospecting . . . in addition to searching for all forms of treasure on beaches and in the waters of the world. These popular forms of treasure hunting should become a regular part of your program. On vacations as you travel around to the various coin hunting areas, keep your eyes open and be alert to other possibilities as they appear . . . and, they will!

How do "*I*" learn more about the principles involved in these other kinds of treasure hunting? You may not be asking yourself this question now. You may think that you have your hands full with coin hunting. But, there will come a time when your interest will expand, and you will ask that question.

The answer lies in an order blank at the end of this book . . . the order blank for additional Ram publications. Roy Lagal and I have published *Modern Treasure Hunting,* which is a complete overview of all the uses of a modern metal detector (which is what I hope you're *already* using to find coins). You might also enjoy either of the *Treasure Hunting Manuals* by Karl von Mueller. If water hunting appeals to you, by all means read my *Treasure Recovery from Sand and Sea.* Read the various treasure hunting magazines. Your opportunities for information are almost limitless.

There will be times when information or a "tip" is passed to you about a treasure, and it will sound too good to pass up. Prepare yourself now to act immediately on these tips when you hear about them. Get to know as much as you can about the other aspects of treasure hunting, if only from a "book-learning" aspect. After all, what does it hurt to strengthen yourself by adding to your store of knowledge?

Expand your horizons. Increase your interests, and enlarge your knowledge of the world through finding wealth with a metal detector. Treasure hunters sometimes develop into rather learned authorities in various aspects of life as it was lived in the past. After all, that's one of the benefits of studying history. One of my interests which developed as an offshoot of treasure hunting is Indian lore. I have surveyed the Comanche war trail which leads from Kansas, down through Oklahoma, New Mexico and Texas into Mexico. I have located several Indian encampments, many artifacts, arrowheads and implements. I discovered the burial sites of two Indian chiefs, one I named "Chief Stone Mountain," and I discovered the location of a three-acre Indian burial ground. I directed local archaeologists to these sites.

My interest in Indians was also directed to the Nez Perce tribe of the Pacific Northwest. This interest has resulted in some delightful excursions with Roy Lagal and other friends in that area as well as the second Gar Starrett novel, *The Missing Nez Perce Gold*. I hope that you will read this tale of a metal detector search for millions of dollars in gold coins which were hidden more than a century ago when the Nez Perce Indians both fought and fled from the U. S. Army. It's an exciting tale I'm certain you will enjoy.

So, you're only interested in coin hunting, you say. Perhaps that's true today. But, give this hobby a little time and see where it leads you . . .

Join Others

No matter what you want to hunt with a metal detector, I strongly recommend that you consider joining one of the many treasure hunting clubs located in America and in other countries. Members are treasure hunters just like you and me who have discovered this great hobby and enjoy the rewards of participating in it. THers have learned that by joining together they can not only increase their pleasure from the benefits of our hobby but help keep it strong by protecting it from damaging legislation on all levels.

Policing the Code of Ethics which you learned about in Chapter 14 is but one of the jobs of these clubs. They vary in size from a just a few members to hundreds. The groups meet regularly for fellowship, to share adventures and to compare their success in the field and water. At the same time, these sincere hobbyists seek knowledge of new developments in the science of metal detecting and try to remain abreast of the rapidly changing laws and regulations that govern their hobby. I know that it's both a pleasure and an honor for me every time I'm invited to appear before one of them!

If you can't find a club locally, write to Garrett headquarters and let us help you find one. Or, better yet, let us help you organize one!

Pays for Itself

To say that coin hunting is a hobby that can truly pay for itself tells only part of the story of this great pastime. Certainly the hobby can repay the cost of its necessary equipment . . . many times over, in fact. Even though the price of a quality modern metal detector might seem somewhat high to a novice, the rewards that come with it can be great indeed. These include not only those rewards of the spirit but actual bounty that can bring immediate financial benefit. When you find a modern coin with no numismatic value, what could be better than spending it at once!

But, there is more to the hobby of coin hunting than financial rewards. Unless you intend to become a professional treasure hunter, we urge that you not undertake this hobby only for the value of those coins and other objects you can find. You'll be missing much of the enjoyment of treasure hunting if you pursue it solely for financial gain – and you'll avoid possible disappointment!

Oh, if you learn your lessons from this book properly, use the right equipment and practice diligently, you'll find plenty of coins or anything you decide to look for . . . be it jewelry, gold nuggets, relics or whatever else. I've seen too many men and women become successful to doubt the potential abilities of anyone. But real success comes only with the joy of the hunt. Gar Starrett is a fictional character I created to tell about some of the exciting treasure hunts in which I have participated. The first two novels, *The Secret of John Murrell's Vault,* and *The Missing Nez Perce Gold,* have just been published. A third, *The Mystery of the Big Bend Treasure Map,* is near completion. At the close of each of these novels, Starrett makes a statement about the hunts just completed. His observation is so pertinent that every treasure hunter should heed it:

"What a delightful treasure hunt it was! But, aren't they all? If nobody gets hurt or spends money he or she can't afford, every treasure hunt is a genuine pleasure."

I couldn't have said it better myself!

In Closing

More than 15 years ago I wrote these final paragraphs and frankly I'm amazed at my prescience. They're just as true today as they were then:

"No final chapter to this book can be written. Detector operator expertise and detector instrumentation are both changing at a fantastic rate. Practice brings improved detector operator skills, and tomorrow will bring advancements in metal detector designs. New places to search will be found; new detector applications will be discovered. This book is only a beginning . . .

"My desire has been to steer you down the road of *Successful Coin Hunting*. Within its pages I have discussed the majority of what is presently known about the coin hunting hobby. Use this information to your best advantage, and, as my good friend Roy Lagal likes to say . . . *'ride out the rest of the trail and enjoy it!'*

"God bless you all . . . "

And, *I'll see you in the field* . . .

Charles Garrett

BOOK ORDER FORM

Please send the following books

☐ **Modern Treasure Hunting**.................$12.95

☐ **Treasure Recovery from Sand and Sea**......$12.95

☐ **Modern Electronic Prospecting**...........$ 9.95

☐ **Buried Treasure of the United States**.......$ 9.95

☐ **Weekend Prospecting**.....................$ 3.95

☐ **The New Successful Coin Hunting**........$10.95

☐ **Modern Metal Detectors**...................$ 9.95

☐ **Treasure Hunter's Manual #6**..............$ 9.95

☐ **Treasure Hunting Pays Off!**...............$ 6.95

☐ **Gold Panning Is Easy**.....................$ 6.95

☐ **Treasure Hunter's Manual #7**..............$ 9.95

☐ **The Secret of John Murrell's Vault**.........$ 2.95

☐ **The Missing Nez Perce Gold**...............$ 2.95

Garrett Guides to Treasure

☐ **Find An Ounce of Gold a Day**.............$ 1.00

☐ **Metal Detectors Can Help You Find Wealth**...$ 1.00

☐ **Find Wealth on the Beach**.................$ 1.00

☐ **Metal Detectors Can Help You Find Coins**...$ 1.00

☐ **Find Wealth in the Surf**...................$ 1.00

☐ **Find More Treasure With the Right Detector** $ 1.00

☐ **Money Caches Are Waiting to be Found**.....$ 1.00

☐ **Avoid Detector Problems**..................$ 1.00

Please add 50¢ for each book ordered (to a maximum of $2) for handling charges.

Total for Items $_____

Texas Residents Add 8% Tax $_____

Handling Charge $_____

Total of Above $_____

MY CHECK OR MONEY ORDER $_____
IS ENCLOSED.

I prefer to order through ☐ **VISA**   or ☐ MasterCard

(Check one.)

_____
Card Number

_____
Expiration Date

_____
Phone #

_____
Signature (Order must be signed.)

_____
NAME

_____
ADDRESS

_____
CITY, STATE, ZIP

Ram Publishing Company
P.O. Drawer 38649
Dallas, TX 75238

BOOK ORDER FORM

Please send the following books

- ☐ **Modern Treasure Hunting**..................$12.95
- ☐ **Treasure Recovery from Sand and Sea**......$12.95
- ☐ **Modern Electronic Prospecting**............$ 9.95
- ☐ **Buried Treasure of the United States**........$ 9.95
- ☐ **Weekend Prospecting**......................$ 3.95
- ☐ **The New Successful Coin Hunting**.........$10.95
- ☐ **Modern Metal Detectors**....................$ 9.95
- ☐ **Treasure Hunter's Manual #6**...............$ 9.95
- ☐ **Treasure Hunting Pays Off!**.................$ 6.95
- ☐ **Gold Panning Is Easy**......................$ 6.95
- ☐ **Treasure Hunter's Manual #7**...............$ 9.95
- ☐ **The Secret of John Murrell's Vault**..........$ 2.95
- ☐ **The Missing Nez Perce Gold**...............$ 2.95

Garrett Guides to Treasure

- ☐ **Find An Ounce of Gold a Day**..............$ 1.00
- ☐ **Metal Detectors Can Help You Find Wealth**...$ 1.00
- ☐ **Find Wealth on the Beach**..................$ 1.00
- ☐ **Metal Detectors Can Help You Find Coins**...$ 1.00
- ☐ **Find Wealth in the Surf**....................$ 1.00
- ☐ **Find More Treasure With the Right Detector** $ 1.00
- ☐ **Money Caches Are Waiting to be Found**.....$ 1.00
- ☐ **Avoid Detector Problems**...................$ 1.00

Please add 50¢ for each book ordered (to a maximum of $2) for handling charges.

Total for Items	$	_____
Texas Residents Add 8% Tax	$	_____
Handling Charge	$	_____
Total of Above	$	_____
MY CHECK OR MONEY ORDER IS ENCLOSED.	$	_____

I prefer to order through ☐ **VISA**   or ☐ MasterCard

(Check one.)

_____
Card Number

_____
Expiration Date

_____
Phone #

_____
Signature (Order must be signed.)

_____
NAME

_____
ADDRESS

_____
CITY, STATE, ZIP

Ram Publishing Company
P.O. Drawer 38649
Dallas, TX 75238